MW00453644

THE GREAT TASTE OF SPAIN

COOKBOOK

A DEFINITIVE GUIDE TO A GRANDMA'S HOME COOKING

Marta Ortiz

Text, photography and design:
Marta Ortiz

Editing and proofreading:
Alun Jones

TABLE OF CONTENTS

SPANISH GASTRONOMY AND TAPAS

In Spain, food is essential part of our every day lives. As we Spaniards often say. "We live to eat rather than eat to live." Our country is so rich and diverse on every level and we enjoy an outstanding gastronomy with an enormous wide range of foods and culinary traditions. The gastronomy of Spain is well known all over the world, not only for its excellence but for its high health value as a Mediterranean diet. But it's not only about the food itself. Going out for a "tapeo" (to have tapas), meeting up for an "aperitivo", these are ordinary social activities that revolve around food and literally bring Spanish food alive.

My intention with this cookbook is to introduce you to over 100 authentic Spanish recipes from different regions of Spain and share our traditions, the origins of the recipes and how and when we usually prepare them. In two words: our "culinary culture".

In some of the recipes, you will see a symbol that says "Also a Tapa". This means that you can also serve it in small portions and eat it as a Tapa. But what is a Tapa?, you may ask. The word Tapa comes from the Spanish verb "tapar" which means to cover. It is said that it all started in Andalusia when people who were drinking outdoors came up with the idea of covering their drinks with a slice of bread between sips to keep the flies out of their glass. Tapas have since evolved considerably and now there are several different categories but with one essential thing in common: you must be able to hold them in one hand or eat them in two to three bites. A tapa may be called a pincho in one region of Spain or a montadito in another.

TAPAS SUB-CLASSES:

- Pinchos (Pintxos in Northern Spain refer to any type of tapa): This is a tapa with a *pincho* or toothpick through the middle to keep all the ingredients aligned and together. Most of the time, the base is a slice of bread, but not always. The toothpick also helps keep track of the number of tapas the customer has eaten.
- Banderillas: Small skewer Tapas.
- Montaditos (On top): the base is one or more slices of bread with other ingredients placed on top.
- Cazuelitas (Clay dishes): served in a small clay dish.
- Raciones (Portions): a small plate with a batch of croquettes, squid rings, brave potatoes, potato salad, etc. which can be shared (or not).

 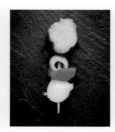   

SPANISH CURED HAM

Since Spanish cured ham is one of the most important food products you can find, in and outside Spain, I thought it would be useful for you to know the different types and qualities of Spanish cured ham. The breed, the amount of exercise and the diet of the pigs have a significant impact on the flavor of the meat. The current labeling system is based on a series of color-coded labels that has been put into place in Spain since January 2014. There are two types of cured ham:

Serrano Ham comes from the white pig breed and its name literally means originating from the "sierra" or mountains.

Ibérico Ham comes from the Iberian pig breed which are black colored and whose meat is much tastier.
At the same time, the Ibérico Ham is classified into the following:

- 100% Ibérico Ham: 100% genetically pure-bred Iberian pigs and both their father and mother are pure-bred
- __% Ibérico Ham: the percentage of Iberian ancestry of the animal must be specified on the label and should be at least 50%.

These 2 types of Ibérico are also sub classified according to the pig's diet and freedom of movement:

A. **De Bellota (Acorn fed)**: Free-range pigs that follow mainly a diet on acorns and grass.
   Iberian piglets are fed on a diet of cereals and acorns until they are nearly 18 months old. The final three months or so of their lives are spent out in the Dehesa (holm oak field) from October to January when acorns fall from the oaks. These pigs need to run around all day through the Dehesa, for their muscles to develop and for the ham to taste the way it does. The pigs must feed on enough acorns to reach 160 kg. The regulations also specify that there should be no more than two pigs per hectare of land to ensure that each pig can eat the required amount of between 6 and 7 kg. of acorns per day. They are sub-classified as:

   - "Pata Negra" (Black Label) if the pig is 100% Ibérico Pure-bred.
   - "Dehesa y Montanera" Red Label if the pig is __% Ibérico Ham .

B. **De Cebo y de Campo** (Green Label): Free-range pigs pastured and fed a combination of grain cereals and none or just a few acorns.
C. **De Cebo (White label):** Not free-range pigs. They are only fed grain. (White label)

The hams are cured at least for 20-24 months. A good *Ibérico* ham has regular flecks of intramuscular fat that look like fine marble. The color is intense and should be shinny. The flesh of the younger hams has a lighter pink color while the longer cured hams have a deeper, ruby red color.

Ibérico Ham shouldn't be sliced by machine. It should be cut by an expert carver to get extra thin, carved at an angle slices that enhance the ham experience in your palate. Some important ham producers, have their pre-sliced packaged ham cut by professional carvers. It really makes a difference. Enjoy!

VEGETABLES

RUSSIAN POTATO SALAD (8)

MALLORCAN VEGETABLE TUMBET (8)

LEVANTE STUFFED COURGETTES (9)

PIPIRRANA (9)

HAM AND MELON (9)

LETTUCE HEARTS TOPPED WITH TUNA VINAGRETTE (10)

ROASTED VEGETABLES - ESCALIVADA (10)

PEAS AND HAM (10)

LA MANCHA PISTO (11)

VEGETABLE STEW NAVARRAN STYLE (11)

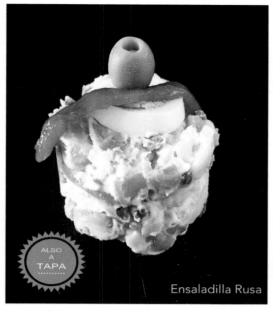

ALSO A TAPA

Ensaladilla Rusa

Pisto Manchego

Peas & Ham

Mallorcan Vegetable Tumbet

Levante Stuffed Courgettes

Escalivada

Lettuce Hearts

Pipirrana

Vegetables Stew Navarran Style

RUSSIAN POTATO SALAD
Ensaladilla Rusa

This recipe dates back to the 19th century, when a Belgian chef, Lucien Olivier, who worked at the Muscovite Restaurant l'Ermitage, invented this salad, which was a great success among the Russian aristocracy. His sous-chef copied this successful recipe and took it with him to another restaurant but that version didn't have much success. Nevertheless, that copy served as a basis for today's recipe, which has become so popular that it has been included in the national Spanish gastronomy.

SERVES 4-6 AS A STARTER OR 10-12 AS A TAPA:
450 gr. (15.5 oz.) potatoes
2 large carrots (180gr./6 oz.)
100 gr. (3.5 oz.) frozen peas
1 hardboiled egg
120 gr. (4.3 oz.) canned tuna in olive oil (optional)
350 ml. (1 ½ cup) mayonnaise (recipe on page 79)
salt to taste
For Decoration:
6-8 green or/and black olives
4-6 roasted red pepper strips
1 hardboiled egg

1. Peel and wash the potatoes and carrots. Cut the potatoes into small square dices about 2 cm. (1 inch) and the carrots into 3 mm. (1/9 inch) thick slices. Then, cut the carrot slices in half.
2. Bring a pot with water and 1 Tbsp. of salt to the boil. Add the potatoes and simmer for 8 minutes. Add in the carrots and peas. Bring into a boil and then lower the heat to simmer for 12-15 min. or until vegetables are tender. Take all the vegetables out with a slotted spoon and place them into a strainer.
3. Boil 2 eggs (see page 80). Finely chop one egg and slice the other one for decoration.
4. When the vegetables in the strainer are cooled, place them in a large tray or plate. Mix in the chopped egg. Optionally add drained and flaked tuna and mix it until well combined.
5. Add the mayonnaise (homemade recipe on page 79). You can either spread a thick layer of mayonnaise on top or you can mix it until well combined with all the ingredients. Use the olives, egg slices and pepper strips as decoration on top. Refrigerate for at least 3 hours covered with cling film. Serve cold but take out of the fridge 15 minutes before serving.

TIP: You can use more ingredients such as sliced or chopped fresh tomatoes, chopped fresh lettuce, boiled green beans or even boiled shrimps.

MALLORCAN VEGETABLE TUMBET
Tumbet Mallorquín

This recipe originally comes from the Balearic Island of Mallorca and it was a way to use up the surplus of seasonal vegetables. It can be eaten on its own as a first course or as a side dish with meat or fish. Originally, the eggplant wasn't peeled for this recipe, but nowadays, many people peel it.

SERVES 4:
1 kg. (2.2 lb.) ripe peeled tomatoes
2 large eggplants
3 medium potatoes
2 large green peppers
1 onion cut into rings
salt to taste
2 tsp. brown sugar
Spanish extra virgin olive oil

1. Cut the eggplants crosswise into thin round slices. Leave them to soak in a bowl of salted water for 30 min. to get rid of the bitterness. Wash and dry the slices. Fry them in hot oil and set aside on a plate lined with kitchen roll.
2. Peel the potatoes, cut them crosswise into thin round slices and wash under cold water. Dry them and season with salt. Fry in hot oil and set aside on a plate lined with kitchen roll.
3. Cut the green peppers lengthwise into 1 cm. (1/3 inch) thick strips. Fry in the same oil where you fried the potatoes until tender. Set aside like before.
4. Fry the onion in the same oil until it looks translucent. Add the finely diced tomatoes and pour 50 ml. (1.8 fl. oz.) water. Season with salt to taste and 2 tsp. brown sugar to get rid of the tomato acidity. Simmer gently uncovered until the sauce has reduced. You can pass the sauce through a sieve if you want. Set aside.
5. Use a deep oven tray to assemble the dish: Place a bit of the tomato sauce and then a layer of the peppers. Put on top more sauce and then a layer of potatoes, more sauce and then a layer of eggplants and so forth until you use up all ingredients.
6. Bake in pre-heated oven at 190ºC (375ºF) for 15 minutes on middle rack and serve immediately.

LEVANTE STUFFED COURGETTES Calabacines Rellenos estilo Levante

This recipe comes originally from the Spanish area of Levante (Mediterranean Coast) and it is a very tasty way to prepare courgettes. It's an ideal first course.

SERVES 4:
4 medium courgettes
2 beaten eggs
80 gr. (3 oz.) diced cured ham
1 medium onion, finely minced
125 ml. (1/2 cup). tomato puree
100 gr. (3.5 oz.) white bread guts

1 garlic clove
finely minced parsley or basil leaves
a handful grated cheese
Spanish extra virgin olive oil
salt to taste
milk

1. Leave the bread guts in a small bowl soaking in cold milk. Pre-heat oven to 200°C (355°F).
2. Wash courgettes. Halve them lengthwise. Scoop out pulp and set aside.
3. Boil or steam the courgette shells in a pot or steamer over a medium heat for 10 minutes until tender. Drain and set aside.
4. Fry in the onion, garlic and pulp in a pan with 2 Tbsp. of olive oil over a medium heat until onion and garlic are light golden.
5. Stir in the ham, tomato puree and combine.
6. Press the bread guts in your hands so the milk in them comes out and fold in the pan.
7. Add the eggs and stir well. Season with salt and cook for 2 minutes.
8. Stuff the courgettes with the pan mixture and sprinkle grated cheese on top. Line an oven tray or dish with baking paper and place the courgettes on it. Grill in oven for about 12 minutes or until the topping is golden crisp. Serve warm and decorate with parsley or basil leaves.

CUCUMBER AND PEPPER SALAD Pipirrana

This recipe originally comes from Jaén, an Andalusian region in Southern Spain. It's halfway between a salad and a gazpacho. It's mostly eaten during Summer because it is very refreshing. You can find different versions across Spain, the most common one being with canned tuna in olive oil with a hardboiled egg. Here I'll show you the original recipe.

SERVES 4
1 large cucumber
1 large green pepper
1 large red pepper
2 chives

2 red tomatoes
salt to taste
Spanish extra virgin olive oil
white wine vinegar or apple vinegar

1. Wash all the vegetables. Peel the cucumber and tomatoes (you can deseed them if you want).
2. Finely dice all the vegetables and combine in a large bowl. Pour 3 Tbsp. of olive oil, ½ tsp. of vinegar all over the ingredients. Season with salt.
3. Serve cold.

HAM & MELON Jamón con melón

This recipe dates back to the 16th century. The melon variety most used in Spain is called "piel de sapo" meaning "Toad skin". It's flavor is perfect because it usually has the right amount of sweetness to work perfectly combined with the cured ham. Some other types like the cantaloupe or honeydew melon might be too sweet for this.

SERVES 4:
4 melon slices
8 cured ham slices

1. Slice the melon and place the cured ham on top. As easy as that.
2. Have it as a fresh starter.

LETTUCE HEARTS TOPPED WITH TUNA VINAGRETTE Cogollos a la vinagreta de atún

This Navarran classic uses lettuce hearts as main ingredient. The ones from Tudela (a nice little town on the banks of the Ebro river) have a very characteristic flavor ideal for this dish. However, any lettuce hearts will do as long as they are good quality.

SERVES 4:
2 lettuce hearts
80 gr. (3 oz.) drained canned tuna in
marinade ("escabeche")
½ green bell pepper

½ red bell pepper
1 spring onion
4 Tbsp. Spanish extra virgin olive oil
salt to taste
ground black pepper

1. Wash the lettuce hearts. Cut them in quarters. Dry them by squeezing them carefully or shaking them off.
2. Wash and finely mince all the vegetables. Place them in a bowl. Spoon in the tuna and pour in the oil. Stir with a fork to combine all ingredients well. Place the lettuce hearts on a plate or platter. Season each lettuce heart with salt and ground pepper to taste. Spoon the bowl contents all over the lettuce hearts.

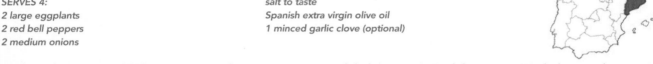

ROASTED VEGETABLES Escalivada

Escalivada is a straightforward vegetable dish that originates from the Catalonian region of Spain. The Catalan word "escalivar" means to roast over ashes or embers. But nowadays, it's usually cooked in an oven with very good results.

SERVES 4:
2 large eggplants
2 red bell peppers
2 medium onions

salt to taste
Spanish extra virgin olive oil
1 minced garlic clove (optional)

1. Pre-heat the oven to 180°C (350°F). Line a large roasting pan with baking paper. Peel the onions. Wash the eggplants, onions and red peppers. Place them on the paper. Cut off the eggplants tails.
2. Make a cross shaped cut with a knife on the bottom of each eggplant. Pour a splash of olive oil all over the vegetables. Roast in oven on middle rack for about 1h 15m, turning over the vegetables every 30 minutes or so. If any vegetables, particularly peppers become thoroughly cooked, while others need more time, remove from tray and continue roasting the rest. Remove from oven and allow to cool.
3. Peel the eggplants when they are cool enough to handle with your hands. Peel the peppers with your hands and discard seeds and stems. Press them all in your hands so the water in them comes out. Cut lengthwise into strips. Place them on a platter or tray.
4. Remove the hard outer layer of the onions. Cut off the edges of the onions if they are black. Cut them into strips and transfer onto the same platter or tray with the rest of vegetables. Pour over a splash of oil and season with salt. You can also sprinkle minced or crushed garlic clove. Serve at room temperature.

PEAS AND HAM Guisantes salteados con jamón

This dish has its origins in Extremadura. It's delicious and yet very simple to make. It makes a great starter or side dish.

SERVES 2
400 gr. (13 oz.) frozen peas
50 gr. (1.7 oz.) Spanish cured ham
1 small onion
1 garlic clove

1 tsp. flour
salt to taste
3 Tbsp. Spanish extra virgin olive oil

1. Boil the peas in water with a pinch of salt for as long as the manufacturer indicates. Drain and set aside. Save and set aside the water in which you boiled the peas. Peel, wash and finely dice the onion. Peel and finely chop one garlic clove. Cut the ham into dices or strips.
2. Pour 3 Tbsp. of olive oil. Add in the onion and garlic and stir fry for 2 minutes over a medium heat. Fold in the ham and cook for 1 minute. Mix in the flour and combine all the other ingredients. Fry for 1 minute.
3. Mix in the peas. Pour in ½ cup of the water in which you boiled the peas and stir. Bring to a gentle boil and cook for 3 minutes. Let it rest for 5 minutes and serve.

LA MANCHA PISTO Pisto Manchego

This is one of the most well-known and popular vegetable dishes in Spain. It is very similar to the French "Ratatouille" and the Italian "Caponata". It has different ingredients depending on the region and the taste of the cook, but it should always have at least tomato, courgette, pepper and onion among its ingredients.

SERVES 4:
400 gr. (13 oz.) courgettes
2 red bell peppers
2 green bell peppers
1 large onion
400 gr. (13 oz.) ripe red tomatoes
Spanish extra virgin olive oil
salt to taste
1 tsp. brown sugar
200 gr. (6 oz.) Spanish cured ham (optional)

1. Wash all the vegetables. Peel and deseed the tomatoes. Cut all the vegetables into small dices, although you can cut the peppers into stripes if you prefer.
2. Heat 3 Tbsp. of olive oil in a large pan over a medium heat. When the oil is hot, turn down to low-medium heat and fry the peppers and onion until tender but not completely cooked (about 5-6 minutes) stirring occasionally. Add in the courgettes and fry until all ingredients are tender and cooked (around 6-7 minutes).
3. Fold in the tomatoes. Sprinkle brown sugar all over the tomatoes to get rid of their acidity. Season with salt, stir and simmer for 15 minutes with a lid on the pan.
4. In case you want to use cured ham, add it in chunks or slices 5 minutes before finishing cooking with the lid off.

VEGETABLE STEW NAVARRAN STYLE Menestra

You can add or substitute any vegetable you like as there's no exact recipe and it can be prepared at any time of the year. The most famous Menestra is the one from the Navarra region. It's usually served as a starter and sometimes potatoes are added to make it more complete.

SERVES 4:
1 medium onion, finely minced
3 artichoke hearts
Spanish extra virgin olive oil
100 gr. (3.5 oz.) Spanish cured ham in dices
200 gr. (6.5 oz.) green beans
3 carrots finely sliced
120 gr. (4.2 oz.) peas
6 white asparagus
350 gr. (12 oz.) potatoes in small dices
3 Tbsp. extra virgin olive oil
salt to taste
optional vegetables: Brussels sprouts, green asparagus, cauliflower and/or broccoli florets

1. Prepare each artichoke. Cut off most of the stalk with a sharp knife. Trim away the top of the artichoke bulb (approx. the top third). Tear off the lower and tougher outer leaves until the yellowy-green center is exposed. With a small sharp knife, trim the tough parts around the stalk. Cut lengthwise into quarters.
2. Use a carrot peeler to take off the outer layer of the asparagus. Wash and set aside.
3. Pour the olive oil into a deep frying pan. Add in and stir fry the artichoke quarters and the ham and onion over a medium heat until the onion is tender.
4. Add the rest of the vegetables, except the asparagus. Give it a good stir. Cover with a lid and simmer over a medium-low heat, stirring occasionally until all vegetables are tender (about 20-25 min.). Stir in the asparagus 5 min. before finishing. If you see it gets too dry, add a little bit of water to prevent the ingredients burning.

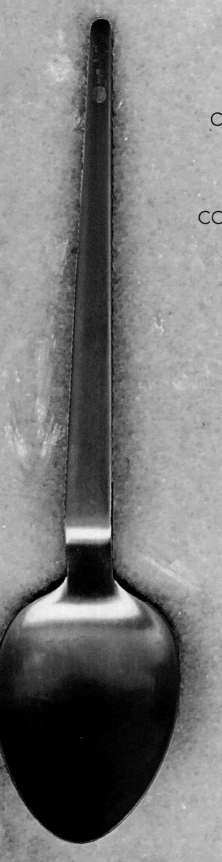

SPOON DISHES

COLD TOMATO SOUP - GAZPACHO (14)

SALMOREJO (14)

CORDOVAN FARMHOUSE CASSEROLE (15)

LENT CHICKPEA STEW (15)

ASTURIAN BEAN CASSEROLE (16)

LEEK SOUP (16)

LENTIL & CHORIZO STEW (17)

GARLIC SOUP CASTILLIAN STYLE (17)

ALMOND AND GARLIC CREME (18)

Cold tomato soup - Gazpacho

Cordovan farmhouse casserole

Salmorejo

Lent chickpea stew

Garlic soup

Almond & garlic creme

Asturian bean casserole - Fabada

Lentil & chorizo stew

Leek soup

COLD TOMATO SOUP Gazpacho

This recipe originally comes from Andalusia in Southern Spain. Nowadays it's the perfect starter to a Summer meal even though Gazpacho was originally served at the end of a meal. Spaniards have it day in, day out during the hot Summer period. It's very refreshing, easy to make, tasty and full of vitamins as it uses fresh vegetables.

SERVES 4:
650 gr. (1.4 lb.) good quality ripe red tomatoes
80 gr. (3 oz.) cucumber
50 gr. (1.7 oz.) green pepper
1 small garlic clove
1 thin slice of white bread
250 ml. (1 cup) ice water
1 tsp. wine vinegar
½ Tbsp. salt
4 Tbsp. Spanish extra virgin olive oil
1 Tbsp. mayonnaise (optional)

1. Cool the vegetables in the fridge for at least 1 hour before making the Gazpacho. Wash all the vegetables. Peel the garlic clove and remove its long core by cutting it lengthwise and then removing it with a knife (see photo on page 79).
2. Peel the cucumber and tomatoes. Pour the water into a blender. Add in all the ingredients chopped up into chunks. They may not fit at once, so you may have to blend them in batches. Blend until the mixture is smooth and pass through a sieve with a large bowl underneath it.
3. Always try it and adjust salt and vinegar to taste.
4. You can either drink it from an individual bowl or eat it with a spoon with sprinkled diced vegetables (cucumber, tomato, onion) and croutons.
5. Serve immediately to take advantage of the vitamins. You could also refrigerate for 1 hour covered with cling film.

TIP: Some top chefs stir in 1 Tbsp. of mayonnaise after the ingredients have been blended.

COLD CORDOVAN TOMATO AND BREAD CREME Salmorejo

This dish originally comes from the Andalusian region of Córdoba. Along with Gazpacho, it is the most popular cold soup in Spain. In fact, many people find Salmorejo more delicious than its famous "cousin". It has influences from the Romans, Greeks and Arabs. It was created as a way to use up stale bread and at first didn't contain tomatoes. Its creaminess is derived from the way the oil and bread emulsify and then fuse with the tomatoes. In Córdoba, it is generally enjoyed by dipping bread or using a spoon.

SERVES 4:
1 kg. (23 oz.) good quality ripe red tomatoes
1 garlic clove
200 gr. (7 oz.). white bread guts
½ Tbsp. salt
125 ml. (1/2 cup) Spanish extra virgin olive oil
3 hardboiled eggs
Spanish cured ham in dices or strips

1. Wash and peel the tomatoes. Circle the stem, then remove the core. Cut into quarters and place in a tall stand up food processor or blender.
2. Peel the garlic clove and remove its long core by cutting it lengthwise and then removing it with a knife (see photo on page 79). Add it into the blender.
3. Blend until the mixture is smooth. Add in the bread and salt. Blend again. While the blender is running, remove the lid and pour in little by little the olive oil. You should get an homogeneous smooth creme. If your blender is not big enough to do it in one go, do it in batches. Try and adjust salt. Refrigerate covered with cling film for at least 1 hour.
4. Meanwhile, hardboil 3 eggs (follow recipe on page 80) and once chilled, cut into small dices. Slice the ham. Use as much as you want as garnish on top along with the diced eggs.

CORDOVAN FARMHOUSE CASSEROLE Olla Cortijera de Córdoba

This dish originally comes from the Andalusian province of Córdoba. It started as a farmhouse food and has become very popular all over the country. It is mostly eaten during the Winter period.

SERVES 4
200 gr. (6.5 oz.) dried chickpeas
1/2 tsp. baking soda
120 gr. (4.2 oz.) onion, finely chopped
1 garlic clove, finely chopped
around 700 gr. (1.5 lb.) cabbage
100 gr. (3.5 oz.) bacon, diced
salt to taste
1 Tbsp. Spanish extra virgin olive oil

1. Soak the chickpeas overnight in water with the baking soda. Pour in enough water taking into account the chickpeas will double in size.
2. The next day, rinse the chickpeas under water and drain. Pour them into a pot with 1.7 liters (7 cups) of warm water. Bring to a boil. With a wooden spoon, skim off any foam that forms on the surface. Add in the onion, garlic and oil.
3. Simmer with the lid on over a medium-low heat for 1 hour.
4. Cut off the stem of the cabbage. Since its chemicals will react with metal, use a stainless steel knife to cut it. Remove the outer layer of soggy leaves and cut the cabbage around the core into smaller pieces. Discard the core. Peel away the leaves and rinse them under water. Break them into smaller pieces with your hands or cut them with a stainless knife.
5. Add the cabbage and bacon into the pot. Season with salt. Simmer for at least 1 more hour with the lid on. At the end, the chickpeas should be tender. They might need more time depending on the hardness of the water and altitude. The water should reduce so it barely covers the chickpeas. If you see there's too much water, cook with the lid off until it's reduced.

LENT CHICKPEA STEW Potaje de Cuaresma

This is a very traditional Spanish Easter dish and it tastes better than you can imagine. There's nothing more typical than having this Potaje on Holy Friday and also on any Friday during "Cuaresma" Lent, the 40 days between Carnival and Easter. If you ever need to re-heat it in the pot, do it slowly so the chickpeas don't break.

SERVES 4
200 gr. (6.5 oz.) dried chickpeas
1 tsp. of baking soda
1 medium onion, finely chopped
2 peeled garlic cloves
200 gr. (6.5 oz.) fresh or frozen cod
200 gr. (6.5 oz.) fresh or frozen spinach
1 toast of bread
1 medium potato
2 bay leaves
salt to taste
4 Tbsp. Spanish extra virgin olive

1. Soak the chickpeas overnight in water with baking soda. Pour in enough water taking into account that the chickpeas will double in size. The next day, rinse the chickpeas under water and drain.
2. Fry the onion and bay leaves in a large pot with 2 Tbsp. olive oil over a medium heat until onion becomes tender.
3. Pour chickpeas into the pot with 1.7 liters (7 cups) of warm water. Bring to a boil and reduce heat to low and simmer covering with a lid. Cook for 1h 30m. Add in the spinach and the cod in small chunks.
4. Fry the garlic and bread in a small frying pan with 2 Tbsp. of oil until golden. Transfer to a mortar and crush with a pestle until you get a paste or blend with a food processor with a drop of the water from the pot. Pour the mixture into the pot. Stir in and bring the chickpeas back to a low boil.
5. Peel and cut the potato into medium size chunks. Salt to taste and simmer for 50 minutes. Then, check if ingredients are tender. They might need more time depending on the hardness of the water or altitude. Also at the end, the water should reduce so that it barely covers the chickpeas.

ASTURIAN BEAN CASSEROLE Fabada Asturiana

"Faba" is the word that refers to the white bean used in this recipe. This is an icon dish from Asturias. Fabada is a consistent dish so it is most commonly eaten during the Winter as the main course. It is typically served with Asturian cider. If you can't find all the ingredients, try making it with what you have available.

SERVES 6
1 kg. (2.2 lb.) large white beans, e.g., lima or butter beans
mineral water with ¼ tsp. of baking soda
120 gr. (4 oz.) chorizo (not spicy hot)
120 gr. (4 oz.) blood sausage or morcilla
120 gr. (4 oz.) of cured ham shoulder (lacón)
120 gr. (4 oz.) slab bacon (panceta)

2 ladles of chicken broth (page 78)
1/2 medium onion, finely chopped
½ tsp. sweet paprika
1 tsp. of saffron threads
6 Tbsp. Spanish extra virgin olive oil

1. Soak the beans overnight in mineral water with the baking soda. Pour in enough water taking into account they will double in size. Do the same with the chorizo, blood sausage, pork and bacon in another bowl with water. The next day, after at least 10 hours, drain the water from both bowls.
2. In a large pot, add the beans and meat products (as a whole, neither cut nor slice) with enough water to cover them. Pour 3 Tbsp. oil and bring to a boil. Skim off any foam that forms on top with a wooden spoon. To avoid breaking the beans, don't stir with a spoon from now on. Just shake the pot with your hands.
3. After 15 minutes, pour in the warm chicken broth (see recipe on page 78). Fry the onion in a small frying pan with 3 Tbsp. oil and when it starts to get tender, add the paprika and fry literally for 3 seconds. Pour the content of the pan into the pot. Add in the saffron. Add 1-2 Tbsp. of salt. Shake the pot with your hands to mix the ingredients. Try it and adjust salt. Cook covered over a low boil for 2 hours until the meat and beans are tender and the cooking liquid is thick and slightly reduced. Let it stand covered for 1 ½ – 2 hours if possible.
4. Remove the bacon and slab ham from the pot and cut them into large pieces. Cut the blood sausages and chorizos into slices. Now you have two options:

    a. Place all the cut meat products back into the pot and then serve individually.
    b. Serve the meat products on a different plate or tray.

TIP: You can boil extra chorizo and blood sausage in a different pot for half an hour if you want more meat to accompany your bean casserole.

LEEK SOUP Porrusalda

The term Porrusalda comes from the Basque words "porru" for leek and "salda" for broth. In the olden days, it used to be a Lent dish and is believed to have humble origins. There is a bit of a controversy over if the dish should include cod among its ingredients or not.

SERVES 4-6
6 leeks
400 gr. (14 oz.). potatoes
2 large carrots (160 gr./5 oz.)
1 medium size onion

1.2 liters (5 cups) water
salt to taste
ground black pepper to taste
2 Tbsp. Spanish extra virgin olive oil

1. Peel and finely chop the onion. Fry in a wide pot with 2 Tbsp. of olive oil over a medium-low heat. When the onion is tender and before it gets golden, pour in the water.
2. Wash the leeks and cut into slices. Then cut them in half. Fold them into the soup. Wash the potatoes and carrots.
3. Cut the potatoes into irregular chunks about 2.5 cm. (1 inch) wide and the carrots into medium thick slices. Mix them into the pot. Add salt and pepper to taste. Simmer covered with a lid for 18-20 minutes. Serve warm.

LENTIL & CHORIZO STEW   Lentejas con chorizo

This is a great dish full of hearty flavor. Spaniards eat it all year around. Simple, healthy, cheap and overall delicious. You can also try making it without the chorizo. If you want to help your body absorb the high iron content of the lentils, accompany with a tomato salad or follow with some fruit rich in vitamin C.

SERVES 4
200 gr. (6.5 oz.) dry brown lentils
½ medium onion, finely chopped
½ green bell pepper, finely chopped
1 small tomato in chunks
2 carrots in slices
1 small potato

2 garlic cloves
80 gr. (3 oz.) Spanish sliced chorizo sausage (not spicy hot)
1 bay leaf
Spanish extra virgin olive oil
splash of white vinegar (optional)
a handful of rice (optional)
salt to taste

1. Heat 2 Tbsp. of oil in a large pot over a medium heat. Add in and fry the bay leaf, finely chopped garlic cloves, onion, green pepper and chorizo until tender.
2. Add the lentils to the pot. Some lentils need soaking for an hour prior to cooking but others don't. It depends on the brand or type of lentils you buy. Check the seller's instructions.
3. Add 1.5 liters (6 cups) of cold water. Add the tomato. Bring to a boil over a high heat. When it starts boiling, pour in half a glass of cold water which will stop the boil. Bring again to a boil and stop it again with half a glass of cold water. Repeat a 3rd time. Put on a lid and simmer for 40 minutes.
4. Cut the carrots into 1/2 cm. (0.2 inch) thick slices. Cut the potato into 2.5 cm (1 inch) thick slices and stir them into the pot. Cook uncovered for 10 minutes. Add salt to taste now and not before, to tender up the lentils quicker.
5. Simmer for 40 minutes over medium-low heat and with the lid on. Add in the rice if using 30 minutes before finishing.
6. Before serving, adjust salt and make sure the lentils are tender. If they are a bit hard, cook longer. Some people like lentils with a splash of white vinegar added just before serving the dish.

GARLIC SOUP CASTILLIAN STYLE   Sopa de ajo castellana

This is an ancient rural dish that originally comes from the Castillian region of Spain, which is "the land of bread". It's a very warming soup for cold Winter days.

SERVES 2
4 slices (1-1.5 cm/ 0.4-0.6 inches thick) of stale bread
1 garlic clove, finely sliced
1 tsp. sweet paprika
600 ml. (2 ½ cup) warm water
1 bay leaf
salt to taste
ground black pepper to taste
Spanish extra virgin olive oil

1. Fry 2 slices of bread in a small pan with 2 Tbsp. olive oil until golden on both sides and set aside.
2. Heat 2 Tbsp. olive oil in a casserole or pot and fry both sides of the other 2 bread slices along with the garlic. Fry over a medium heat for 2 minutes stirring ocasionally.
3. Remove the casserole or pot from the heat and sprinkle the paprika on the bread. Stir and combine.
4. Pour in the warm water. Add a bay leaf. Simmer covered for 25 minutes.
5. Top the soup with the 2 bread slices that you fried on step 1. Let them float and wait till they get soggy.
6. Try the soup and adjust salt and pepper to taste.

TIP: For more flavor and protein, you can break an egg into each bowl at the end of the preparation and bake it in the oven until the egg is set. You could also poach an egg in the soup itself for 3 minutes.

ALMOND AND GARLIC CREME   Ajo Blanco

There is an ownership dispute between the Málaga and Granada regions of Andalusia over it origins, both claiming it. The term "Ajo Blanco" means "White Garlic" in Spanish and it refers to one of the main ingredients and the color of this dish. The old basic recipe didn't use any bread but the modern one includes it amongst its ingredients.

SERVES 4
150 gr. (5 oz.) stale crusty bread guts
3 garlic cloves
100 gr. (3.5 oz.) skinless almonds
75 ml. (5 Tbsp.) Spanish extra virgin olive oil
1/2 Tbsp. white wine vinegar
salt to taste
For Decoration:
green grapes cut in half lengthwise melon slices
(optional)
Spanish cured ham in strips (optional)
croutons (optional)

1. Cut the bread into chunks and soak them in water until tender. (Around 15-25 minutes depending on the type of bread).
2. Bring 1 liter (4 cups) of water to a boil and pour in the almonds. Stir well until it boils again and cook for 30 seconds.
3. Take out the almonds with a strainer and place on kitchen roll to get rid of the water. Set the water aside. Let the almonds cool.
4. Put all the ingredients except the oil in a blender and add in 2 cups (500 ml.) of the water where you boiled the almonds. Blend for a minute until you get a smooth paste. While the blender is still on, take off the little lid and pour alternatively and little by little the olive oil and the remaining water set aside. Blend until you get a creamy soup.
5. Oil and water measures are approximate, so use as much as you need for a creamy soup consistency.
6. Try and adjust salt to taste. Put in the fridge covered with cling film for at least 1 hour. Serve decorated with green grapes, melon, ham and/or croutons.

EGGS

SPANISH POTATO OMELETTE (22)

TUNA STUFFED EGGS (23)

OPEN EGGS WITH GREEN ASPARAGUS (23)

BROKEN EGGS (23)

GIRALDA EGGS (24)

MUSHROOM AND SHRIMP SCRAMBLED EGGS (24)

GALICIAN WITCHES' OMELETTE (24)

CARLISTAS EGGS (25)

COD OMELETTE (25)

Open eggs with green asparagus

Giralda eggs

Broken eggs with cured ham

Spanish potato omelette

Mushroom & shrimp scrambled eggs

Galician witches' omelette

Tuna stuffed eggs

Carlistas eggs

Cod omelette

SPANISH POTATO OMELETTE Tortilla de Patata

This is one of the most famous Spanish recipes. The one here includes onions but you could also make it without. There are many variations which contain different ingredients, like sliced chorizo, ham, zucchini, peppers, etc.

MAKES 1 LARGE OMELETTE FOR 3-4 PEOPLE: 5 large beaten eggs – 3 medium potatoes - 1 medium onion - Spanish olive oil - salt to taste

1. Wash the potatoes under running water. Peel them and <u>do not wash</u> them again. Cut into thin half slices.
2. Peel, wash and finely chop the onion. Use a 23 cm. (9 inch) based pan. Heat 3-4 lugs of olive oil over a medium heat. Wait until the oil is hot and then carefully add the potatoes and onion. The oil should at least cover the bottom half of the potatoes. Season with salt. Cover with a lid and fry over medium-low heat while stirring occasionally.
3. After 7 minutes, break the potatoes with a wooden spatula in the pan. Stir well and cover. Fry until completely done (around 20 min.). Take out the potato and onion mixture with a slotted spoon or ladle and place in a sieve with a bowl underneath so the oil drips into it.
4. Place eggs in a large bowl and add 2 pinches of salt. Beat by hand and add the potato onion mixture. Combine.
5. You will cook the omelette in a smaller and non-stick 20 cm. (8 inch) based pan. You could also use an even smaller pan to make a smaller but thicker omelette. Pour 1 Tbsp. of the remaining olive oil from the bowl into the pan and heat over a medium heat. When the oil is hot, but before smoking hot, pour the potato-egg mixture into the pan. Spread out evenly. Move the pan around. If some parts of the omelette don't move, this means it has stuck to the pan. Using a non-stick spatula, scrape underneath the bottom. Cover the frying pan with a lid and allow the omelette to cook around the edges over a <u>low heat</u> (about 8 min. depending on the size of the pan).
6. Find a plate which is larger than the pan and place it upside down over the pan. Hold the handle with one hand and the top of the plate with the other.
7. Quickly flip the pan over and the omelette will "fall" onto the plate. Place the pan back on the heat and pour a quick splash of olive oil into the pan.
8. Carefully slide the omelette into the frying pan. Use the spatula to flatten the sides of the omelette. Let it cook covered over a low heat for 5-6 minutes. Turn the heat off and let it sit in the pan for 2 minutes.
9. Slide the omelette onto a large plate to serve. It can be a main course or a tapa.

TUNA STUFFED EGGS

Huevos rellenos de atún

This recipe is quite similar to the popular Deviled Eggs. They are usually served as a starter or a tapa.

FOR 8 STUFFED EGGS
4 eggs
150 gr. (5.2 oz.) drained canned tuna in flakes
1 large lettuce leaf
2 Tbsp. mayonnaise (see page 79)
salt to taste

1. Hardboil the eggs following recipe on page 80.
2. Slice each egg in half.
3. Gently remove the yolk halves and place in a small bowl. Arrange the egg white halves on a serving platter.
4. Wash and finely chop the lettuce leaf.
5. Mix the lettuce with the yolks in the bowl. Using a fork, mash up everything.
6. Add the mayonnaise (recipe on page 79) and a pinch of salt. Toss in the drained tuna and combine. Spoon the bowl mixture into the egg white halves. Refrigerate for at least an hour.

OPENED EGGS WITH GREEN ASPARAGUS

Huevos abiertos con espárragos verdes

Typical egg recipe from the Aragonese region. Some versions use white instead of green asparagus and add cured ham.

SERVES 4:
4 eggs
3 garlic cloves, finely minced
100 gr. (3.5 oz.) green asparagus
100 gr. (3.5 oz.) rice
2 Tbsp. flour
50 ml. (3 Tbsp). extra virgin olive oil
500 ml (2 cups) vegetable broth or water
ground parsley and salt
a pinch of orange food coloring (optional)

1. Pour the oil in a XL pan and heat over a medium heat. When hot, fry the garlic until light golden.
2. Add the flour and fry for 1 minute.
3. Pour the water or broth and bring to a boil. Use a carrot peeler to take off the outer layer of the asparagus. Stir them and the rice into the boiling broth. As soon as you stir them in, the boiling will stop. Keep the heat high and wait for a second boil.
4. Season with salt. Lower the heat to medium-low and cover with a lid. Simmer for 15 minutes. Add the food coloring (if using) and mix.

5. Crack the eggs one by one onto a plate. Gently slide in one egg at a time. Sprinkle salt over the eggs. Use a spoon to push some of the egg whites closer to their yolks. Cover and simmer for 10 minutes. Sprinkle parsley on top and serve.

BROKEN EGGS Huevos Rotos

This is a dish you'll find in any Spanish restaurant. Spaniards usually eat this for lunch or dinner but never for breakfast. When non-Spaniards try it, they are impressed and it usually becomes one of their favorite Spanish dishes. The original version only has potatoes and eggs. It may sound boring but it's amazingly delicious when properly made. Other versions can also include chorizo, cured ham (this recipe), blood sausage, fried green peppers, fried shrimps and even foie gras.

SERVES 2
4 eggs
700 gr. (1.5 lb.) potatoes
Spanish extra virgin olive oil
salt to taste
4 slices of Spanish cured ham cut into strips

1. Peel the potatoes. Wash and cut into slices. Wash again under running water to get rid of the starch. Heat up olive oil in a large frying pan. The oil should at least cover the bottom half of the potato slices. Place them into the hot oil and fry over a medium heat, stirring frequently. Add salt to taste. Remove with a slotted spoon when they turn light golden brown, after about 12 minutes. Set aside to cool on a paper towel lined plate.
2. Crack one egg onto a plate and season with salt.
3. Pour the left over oil used to fry the potato slices, into a small non-stick frying pan. There should be a good amount of oil (1 finger deep). Heat it over a medium-high heat until it begins to smoke.
4. Carefully slip the egg into the oil and immediately turn the heat down to low. Fry until edges of the egg white are golden. Tilt the frying pan and pour oil from the pan over the egg with a ladle or spoon, in order to also fry the top. Nevertheless, don't pour hot olive oil over the egg yolk if you like it runny. Repeat again for every egg.
5. Place the potato slices on a plate or small paellera. Using a slotted spoon, lift out the eggs and transfer on top of the potatoes. Place the ham strips on top. Break the eggs using 2 spoons and serve immediately.

GIRALDA EGGS Huevos a la Giralda

This recipe is named after the "Giralda" bell tower of the Seville Cathedral, whose construction was finished in 1189. This Andalusian recipe can be modified by changing the vegetables to suit your taste.

SERVES 4
4 eggs
2 medium onions, finely chopped
4 medium tomatoes, peeled and finely chopped
2 small green bell peppers, finely chopped
2 small red bell peppers, finely chopped
3 garlic cloves, finely minced
a splash of vinegar
salt to taste
½ Tbsp. sugar
1 ½ Tbsp. Spanish extra virgin olive oil

1. Fry the onions, peppers and garlic until tender in a deep frying pan with oil over a medium-low heat.
2. Add the tomatoes, sugar and salt to taste. Combine well and simmer with a lid on for 15 minutes over a low heat.
3. To poach the eggs, heat 5 cm. (2 inches) of water in a small pot over a medium-high heat. Pour a splash of vinegar. Crack one egg into a plate and slide it into the boiling water. If the yolk brakes, then discard it. Repeat with the remaining eggs. Leave room between the eggs, preparing in two, three or single batches if need be. Cook eggs, undisturbed, until white is just set and yolk is still runny, approx. 3 to 4 minutes. Gently use a spatula to release eggs from the bottom of the pan, if necessary.
4. Using a slotted spoon, remove each egg from water and transfer to individual dishes. Cover each egg with the vegetables from the pan and serve.

MUSHROOM & SHRIMP SCRAMBLED EGGS

Huevos revueltos con setas y gambas

Spaniards have a way with eggs. They love them scrambled but they will rarely have them for breakfast. This dish is very simple and easy to prepare but it is served in Spanish homes at lunch, dinner or as a tapa.

SERVES 4
8 large eggs, beaten
600 gr. (21 oz.) mushrooms or any type of funghi
300 gr. (11 oz.) peeled raw shrimps
2 garlic cloves, minced
2 Tbsp. Spanish extra virgin olive oil.
salt to taste
parsley
ground black pepper

1. Clean the mushrooms or funghi with a damp paper towel or soft brush. You can rinse them lightly under cold water, patting the mushrooms dry or even pressing them between your hands so all the water comes out.
2. Wash the shrimps and also press them between your hands so all the water in them comes out. Cut the mushrooms into thick slices. Set aside.
3. Heat up the olive oil in a large frying pan over a medium heat. Fry the garlic cloves. After 1 minute, add in the mushrooms and shrimps. Fry for 2 minutes.
4. Beat the eggs by hand in a bowl for 1 minute. Season with salt. Pour the eggs all over the ingredients in the pan and stir with a wooden spoon or spatula. Cook for 1 minute stirring constantly.
5. Sprinkle with black pepper and parsley.

GALICIAN WITCHES' OMELETTE

Tortilla de las Meigas

This recipe is named after witches in Galicia.

FOR 2 SINGLE OMELETTES
4 eggs
½ medium onion finely minced
50 gr. (1.7 oz.) cured ham strips or dices
75 ml. (5 Tbsp.) tomato puree
handful of grated cheese
For the Bechamel:
flour
milk
olive oil, or melted margarine/butter
salt

1. Fry the onion in 1 Tbsp. of olive oil until golden. Pour in the tomato puree and ham. Stir and fry for 3 minutes over a medium heat. Set aside.
2. To make each individual omelette, place 2 eggs in a bowl and add 1 pinch of salt. Beat by hand.
3. Heat 1 Tbsp. of olive oil over a medium heat in a small frying pan. Wait until the oil is hot and then pour in the beaten eggs. Add half of the tomato filling in the middle. Fold the omelette to wrap the filling. Place in an oven tray. Repeat process with the remaining ingredients to make the other omelette.
4. Make the classic bechamel (see page 80). Cover the omelettes with the bechamel. Top with grated cheese and grill in pre-heated oven at 180° (360°F) for 10 minutes until cheese is golden brown.

CARLISTAS EGGS Huevos Carlistas

The origin of both the name and the recipe is a mystery, but what we know for sure is that they are delicious. The classic version uses fried eggs but you could also use hardboiled ones.

FOR 4 EGGS
6 eggs
Spanish extra virgin olive oil
2 handful of breadcrumbs
50 gr. (5 ½ Tbsp.) all purpose flour
salt and pepper
For the Bechamel:
½ liter (2 cups) milk
50 gr. (1/4) cup olive oil, or melted margarine/butter
50 gr. (5 ½ Tbsp.) all purpose flour
salt to taste

1. Fry 4 eggs following Step 3 and 5 of recipe Broken Eggs on page 23. If you also fry the egg yolk, handling the fried egg in following steps, will be easier. Set aside and let cool. Alternatively, you can hard boil them following recipe on page 80.
2. Prepare the thick bechamel with the quantities indicated on this recipe following the Thick bechamel recipe on page 80. Set aside and refrigerate for 1 hour.
3. Place a handful of cool thick bechamel on one hand and then place the fried egg in the middle. Cover the egg using another handful of bechamel with the other hand. Cover the egg completely and set aside. Repeat process for every egg.
4. Prepare 3 plates: one with flour, another with 2 beaten eggs and the last one with breadcrumbs.
5. Roll each egg in the flour, shaking off any excess.
6. Press each egg on the plate with the beaten eggs and dip it. With a fork, roll them so they are completely coated by the egg.
7. Lift it out of the beaten egg and roll in the bread crumbs coating each egg evenly.
8. Heat up a good amount of olive oil in a frying pan over a high-medium heat. The amount of oil depends on the size of the pan. The oil must cover the bottom half of the eggs and be quite hot at first. When it's hot (but before getting smoky hot) place them carefully in the oil. Lower the heat to a medium heat. Fry them in small batches. Turn them gently, for about 2 minutes, or until they are golden on all sides.
9. Using a slotted spoon, lift out the eggs, holding them briefly over the pan to allow excess oil to drain, and transfer to a paper towel lined plate to drain further. Serve warm.

COD OMELETTE Tortilla de Bacalao

This recipe comes from the Basque Country and it was a favorite fisherman's food. Nowadays it is a must in every good cider house (Sidrería) menu in the Basque Country.

SERVES 4 (1 LARGE OMELETTE)
400 gr. (14 oz.) desalted or fresh cod fillets
6 eggs
½ green bell pepper
1 large onion
2 garlic cloves
Spanish extra virgin olive oil
salt to taste

1. Finely chop the garlic, onion and green peppers. Fry in a pan with 2 Tbsp. olive oil. Season with salt.
2. Flake the cod fillets with a fork.
3. When vegetables are tender and golden, add in the flaked cod and cook for 4-5 minutes.
4. Beat the eggs with a pinch of salt in a bowl. Stir in the cod and vegetables from the pan and mix with a fork.
5. Heat up 1 Tbsp. olive oil in a medium frying pan. When the oil is hot, but before smoking hot, pour the contents of the bowl into the pan. Spread out evenly. Move the pan around. If some parts of the omelette don't move, this means it has stuck to the pan. Using a nonstick spatula, scrape the bottom underneath. Cover the frying pan with a lid and allow the omelette to cook around the edges over a low heat (about 5 min. depending on the size of the pan).
6. Find a plate which is larger than the pan and place it upside down over the pan. Hold the handle with one hand and the top of the plate with the other.
7. Quickly flip the pan over and the omelette will "fall" onto the plate. Place the pan back on the heat and pour a quick splash of olive oil into the pan.
8. Carefully slide the omelette into the frying pan. Use the spatula to flatten the sides of the omelette. Let it cook covered over a low heat for 3-4 minutes. Turn the heat off and let it sit in the pan for 2 minutes. Serve immediately.

PASTA

NOODLE PAELLA - FIDEUÀ (28)

PENNE WITH CHORIZO (28)

CLAY DISH (29)

MEAT CANNELLONI (29)

Noodle Paella- Fideuà

Penne with chorizo

Meat cannelloni

Clay dish- Greixonera

NOODLE PAELLA Fideuà

The term Fideuà comes from the Spanish word for noodle, "Fideo". This noodle version of Fish and Seafood Paella was invented by Zabalo, who was a cook on board a fishing boat. He often cooked Fish Paella, but the skipper of the boat always ate much more of his fair share, leaving the rest of the crew with little Paella. To make the food less appealing, one day Zabalo decided to substitute the rice for pasta. His trick failed and this recipe quickly caught on among local restaurants in Gandía (Valencia).

SERVES 4
400 gr. (13 oz.) dry short or vermicelli noodles
8 large raw unpeeled shrimps
200 gr. (6 oz.) squid rings
3 garlic cloves
½ green bell pepper
½ small onion
1 small peeled tomato
1 liter (4 cups) fish stock (page 78)
1/2 tsp. saffron threads or food coloring for paella
½ tsp. sweet paprika
Spanish extra virgin olive oil
6 Norway Lobsters, 6 mussels and 12 clams (optional)
aioli (see recipe on page 79)
a

1. Use a paella pan (paellera) which is a large flat open round pan with handles or a large electric skillet or pan with a base at least 40 cm. (15-16 inches) wide.
2. Prepare fish stock following the recipe on page 78. Coat the pan with 4 lugs of olive oil. Fry the shrimps on both sides over a medium heat until pink. Season with salt. Remove them from the pan and set aside.
3. Finely chop the green pepper, garlic and onion and fry in the pan until done.
4. Mix in the squid and cook for 3 min. Add the diced tomato and season with salt and paprika. Cook with a lid on for 5 min, stirring frequently.
5. Add the noodles and fry for about 5 min. over a medium heat, stirring constantly.
6. Pour the fish stock and bring to a boil over medium heat. Cook covered for 8 min. Add the saffron threads or a pinch of food coloring.
7. Arrange the seafood (fried shrimps too) in the pan pushing every piece into the noodles. Simmer covered until liquid is absorbed and noodles are done.
8. Remove pan from the heat, cover and let stand for 5 minutes. Noodles should be cooked but firm.
9. It's usually served with aioli on the side.

PENNE WITH CHORIZO
Macarrones con chorizo

Spaniards love pasta and this recipe is very popular in many Spanish homes. There's nothing more typical than having this pasta as a main dish on a Saturday. It's a celebration for everybody, not only for children. It's very tasty and easy to make. It also only takes a few minutes to prepare. If you are in a hurry, this is the recipe for you.

SERVES 4
350 gr. (12 oz.) penne or similar pasta
120 gr. (4.2 oz.) mild Spanish chorizo sausage, sliced
80 gr. (3 oz.) cured loin of pork (optional)
3 slices of cured ham into strips (optional)
1 onion
½ green bell pepper
450 ml. (15 fl. oz.) fried tomato puree
200 ml. (7 fl. oz.) milk
30 ml. (2 Tbsp.) Spanish extra virgin olive oil
2 handfuls of grated cheese
salt to taste

1. Pre-heat oven to 220°C (425°F).
2. Bring a large pot of salted water to a boil. Add the pasta and boil according to package instructions. When done, drain off the water and set pasta aside.
3. While the pasta is boiling, you can start preparing the sauce. Chop the cured loin of pork, if you are also going to add it. Slice the chorizo and finely chop the onion and green pepper. Pour the olive oil into a large frying pan and heat over a medium-low heat. Once hot enough, fry the chorizo, pork, cured ham strips, onion and pepper until cooked (about 5 min.). Stir frequently. Mexican chorizo is not a good substitute for Spanish chorizo due to the different spices they use.
4. Pour in the tomato puree and milk. Season with salt and stir well. Cover and simmer for about 8 minutes.
5. Spoon the pasta into the frying pan and mix together with the sauce. Pour everything into a baking dish. You can also place the pasta first on the baking dish and then pour the sauce all over it and mix.
6. Top with grated cheese and grill in the pre-heated oven for 10 minutes until cheese is light golden brown.

CLAY DISH Greixonera

The name of this dish comes from the Mallorcan word for the clay dish in which it is served. A very unusual recipe as it is a savory dish with cinnamon. Nevertheless, you'll see how well the cinnamon brings out the flavors of the other ingredients.

SERVES 4
a handful of Mahon cheese or Emmental if you can't find it
350 gr. (12 oz.) penne or similar pasta
150 gr. (5.2 oz.) grated
100 gr. (3.5 oz.) butter
250 ml. (1 cup) milk
1 tsp. ground cinnamon
4 hardboiled eggs
salt to taste

1. Pre-heat oven to 220°C (425°F).
2. Hard boil the eggs following recipe on page 80.
3. Bring a large pot of salted water to a boil. Add the pasta and boil according to package instructions. When done, drain off the water and set pasta aside.
4. Warm up the milk in a pot, add in the pasta and simmer until the milk reduces.
5. Sprinkle ¾ of the cheese, ¾ tsp cinnamon and a 1 tsp. of salt. Combine well with a spoon. Pour the pasta into a large clay dish or small individual clay dishes. You can also use any other type of oven dish.
6. Top with the remaining cheese and ¼ tsp. of cinnamon.
7. Place the hardboiled eggs, peeled and in quarters on top. Top every egg with a bit of butter and then spread the remaining butter in small chunks on top of the pasta.
8. Grill in the pre-heated oven for 10 minutes until cheese is light golden brown. Serve immediately.

MEAT CANNELLONI Canelones de Carne

Cannelloni or Manicotti were first introduced into Spain by Italians in the Catalan region. That's why there is a tradition in Catalonia to celebrate the 26th of December with "Canelones". I would recommend using precooked pasta sheets if you can find them, so you can skip boiling them. You can also buy tube pasta which is easier to find in some countries.

SERVES 4
24 pre-cooked cannelloni sheets
500 gr. (17 oz.) minced pork or veal
1 small onion finely chopped
160 gr. (5.5 oz.) foie gras
150 ml. (5.1 fl. oz.) milk
1 Tbsp. wheat flour
Spanish extra virgin olive oil
salt to taste
a handful of grated cheese
For the classic bechamel:
1 liter (4 cups) milk
100 gr. (1/2 cup) butter
100 gr. (3.5 oz.) wheat flour
salt to taste

1. Pre-heat oven to 200°C (392°F).
2. Place the pasta sheets in warm water for 30 min. moving them occasionally or follow the manufacturer's instructions.
3. Fry the meat and onion in a large pan with olive oil over a medium heat. Cook until done.
4. Add the foie gras and combine well. If the meat gets too dry, you can pour in a little oil.
5. Mix in the flour and cook for 2 min. Pour in the milk and season with salt. Stir well. Cook for 5 minutes. Remove from heat.
6. For the classic bechamel, follow recipe on page 80.
7. Take the pasta sheets out of the water and lay on a clean surface. Spoon the filling in a line down center of each sheet and roll them with your hand.
8. Line an oven tray with baking paper and place the cannelloni with the seam facing side down.
9. Top the cannelloni with the bechamel sauce.
10. Sprinkle with grated cheese and grill in oven for 10-15 minutes at 200°C. If you use dry tube pasta, cook in the oven at 180°C (350°F) for 30 minutes before grilling.

RICE

ORIGINAL VALENCIAN PAELLA (32)

MIXED PAELLA (33)

SEAFOOD PAELLA (34)

RICE ON THE SIDE (35)

CUBAN STYLE RICE (35)

BLACK RICE (36)

POTATOES WITH RICE (36)

Black rice

Original Valencian Paella

Seafood Paella

Mixed Paella

Rice on the side

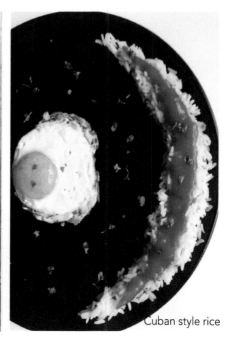

Cuban style rice

ORIGINAL VALENCIAN PAELLA Paella Valenciana

This is the original and genuine Paella recipe. It might come as surprise to you, but it has neither seafood nor chorizo amongst its ingredients. It originated in the 18ᵗʰ century and it was a typical farmers' and farm laborers' food. Made with whatever ingredients were at hand around the rice fields and local countryside: rice, tomatoes, snails, beans and other vegetables, and also meats like chicken or rabbit. Paella was also traditionally eaten straight from the pan with each person using their own wooden spoon.

SERVES 4-5
400 gr. (13 oz.) bomb or round rice
400 gr. (13 oz.) chicken in chunks
400 gr. (13 oz.) rabbit in chunks
2 large artichokes
50 gr. (1.7 oz.). flat green beans
3 garlic cloves
½ green bell pepper
12 lima beans ("garrofó" beans)
1 small peeled tomato
1 liter of chicken broth (see page 78)
1/2 tsp. saffron threads or food coloring for paella
½ tsp. sweet paprika
salt to taste
Spanish extra virgin olive oil

1. Use a paella pan (paellera) which is a large flat open round pan with handles or a large electric skillet or pan with a base at least 40 cm (15-16 inches) wide.T he key for a proper Paella is cooking the rice evenly spread in a thin layer all round the pan in order to absorb all the flavors from the other ingredients. That's why a wide pan is a must.
2. Heat 4 lugs of oil in the paellera. Season with salt the meat and fry until golden brown on the outside. Remove meat and set aside. It doesn't matter if the meat is still raw on the inside at this point. Choose the pieces of meat you prefer. I prefer to use meat pieces with bones. The more bones, the more taste they will add to the recipe.
3. Clean artichokes following method in step 1 of the recipe VEGETABLE STEW NAVARRAN STYLE on page 11. Finely chop the green pepper. Fry the artichokes and green pepper over a medium heat. When they're almost done (soft), stir in the finely chopped garlic cloves and flat green beans.
4. Cut the tomato into small chunks and stir into the pan. Sprinkle the sweet paprika.
5. Add in the lima beans. Season with ¼ tsp. salt and mix well. This mixture is called "sofrito". Gently cook the mixture for 5 minutes in the center of the paellera, stirring frequently.
6. Put all the meat you had set aside earlier back into the paella. Pour in the chicken broth (recipe on page 78) or water and bring to a boil. Add the rice, spreading equally. Bring to a boil again and adjust the heat to maintain a vigorous simmer uncovered for about 5 minutes.
7. Put the saffron threads into a mortar and crush them into dust. Pour 1 Tbsp. of broth from the Paella into the mortar. Mix it with the saffron dust and stir well. Pour the resulting orange liquid into the paellera. If you can't find saffron, you can use 1 tsp. of orange coloring adding directly into the Paella.
8. Cover with a lid and lower to medium-low heat so it reduces to a gentle boil. From now on, don't disturb or stir the rice. Move the paellera around as much as you want to even out the heat, but <u>don't stir the rice</u>. Check the liquid from time to time and add more water if the rice looks dry. It will take 15-20 minutes in total to fully cook. If the paellera has been set over two burners or heat rings, cover it with foil for the last 2 minutes of cooking to ensure the rice cooks evenly.
9. The rice should be dry and separate easily when done, not creamy like risotto. Once cooked, remove the Paella from the heat. If the rice is still a bit hard, you can cover the paellera with a damp cloth and let it rest for 10 min. If it's fully cooked, let it rest uncovered. You can also place the paellera uncovered in a heated oven at 425°F (215°C) for the last 10 minutes of cooking.
10. The crunchy crust of rice that sticks to the bottom of the paellera is the "reward" from a well-made Paella and is called the "Socarrat".

MIXED PAELLA Paella Mixta

Mixed Paella originally comes from the Valencian region on the Eastern Coast of Spain. It combines meat and seafood and is one of the most popular Paella recipes in Spain, especially amongst tourists. It's a Spanish icon all over the world because of its spectacular flavor. But did you know that Paella does not contain chorizo? If you see a Paella with chorizo in it, then it's not a genuine Paella. I was born and raised in Valencia and I've only ever known real Paella recipes. I'm astonished when I see Paella even in other Spanish regions, with chorizo!

SERVES 4
350 gr. (12 oz.) bomb or round rice
600 gr. (21 oz.) of meat such as chicken or rabbit
50 gr. (1.7 oz.). green beans
200 gr. (6 oz.) squid rings
3 garlic cloves, finely minced
½ green bell pepper
1 small peeled tomato
½ small onion, diced
50 gr. (1.7 oz.) frozen peas
900 ml. (3 ½ cups) chicken broth or water
6 large raw shrimps/prawns, unpeeled
12 mussels (optional)
12 clams (optional)
6 Norway lobsters (optional)
1/2 tsp. saffron threads or food coloring for paella
½ tsp. sweet paprika
salt to taste
Spanish extra virgin olive oil

1. Use a paella pan (paellera) which is a large flat open round pan with handles or a large electric skillet or pan with a base at least 40 cm. (15-16 inches) wide.
2. Heat 3 Tbsp. of oil and fry the meat until golden brown on the outside. Season with salt. Remove meat and set aside. It doesn't matter if the meat is still raw on the inside at this point. Choose the meat you prefer. I like to use several types of meat. I also prefer to use meat pieces with bones. The more bones, the more taste they will add to the recipe.
3. Fry the shrimps and Norway lobsters (optional) for 1 minute on each side, take them out and set aside. Fry the garlic over medium heat for 1 minute. Finely chop the green pepper and onion and add them in the paellera with the garlic. Fry them over medium heat. When they're almost done (soft), stir in the green beans and squid rings.
4. Cut the tomato into small chunks and add it in. Sprinkle the sweet paprika all over.
5. Season with ¼ tsp. salt and mix well. This mixture is called "sofrito". Gently cook the mixture for 5 minutes in the center of the paellera, stirring frequently.
6. Put all the meat you had set aside earlier back into the paella. Pour in the chicken broth (recipe on page 78) or water and bring to a boil. Cover with lid. Lower the heat and simmer for 30 minutes. This will transfer the flavor from the meat into the stock.
7. Put the saffron threads into a mortar and crush them into dust. Pour 1 Tbsp. of broth from the Paella into the mortar. Mix it with the saffron dust and stir well. Pour the resulting orange liquid into the paellera. If you can't find saffron, you can add 1 tsp. of orange coloring directly into the Paella.
8. Stir in the peas and bring to a boil again over a high heat. Pour in the rice and carefully stir, spreading equally. Cover with a lid and lower to a medium-low heat so it boils slowly. From now on, don't touch the rice. Move the paellera around as much as you want to even out the heat, but don't disturb or stir the rice. Check the liquid from time to time and add more water if the rice looks dry. It will take 18-20 minutes to fully cook. After 15 minutes, place the unpeeled shrimps and Norway lobsters (if you're adding them) into the stock. Arrange any optional seafood in the pan pushing every piece into the rice. Simmer covered until liquid is absorbed and rice is done. If the paellera has been set over two burners or heat rings, cover it with foil for the last 2 minutes of cooking to ensure the rice cooks evenly.
9. The rice should be dry and separate easily when done, not creamy like risotto. Once cooked, remove the Paella from the heat. If the rice is still a bit hard, you can cover the paellera with a damp cloth and let it rest for 10 min. If it's fully cooked, let it rest uncovered. You can also place the paellera uncovered in a heated oven at 425°F (215°C) for the last 10 minutes of cooking.
10. The crunchy crust of rice that sticks to the bottom of the paellera is the "reward" from a well-made Paella and is called the "Socarrat".

SEAFOOD PAELLA Paella Marinera

In Valencia, fishermen used to make this version of the original Paella recipe when they were out at sea fishing on board their boats. They changed the original meat ingredients for fish and seafood found easily at sea. That's the history behind "Paella Marinera".

SERVES 4
400 gr. (13 oz.) bomb or round rice
200 gr. (6 oz.) squid rings
3 garlic cloves, finely minced
½ green bell pepper
1 small peeled tomato ,minced
½ small onion, diced
50 gr. (1.7 oz.) frozen peas (optional)
1 liter (4 cups) seafood stock (see page 78)

6 large raw shrimps/prawns, unpeeled
12 mussels
12 clams
6 Norway lobsters (optional)
1/2 tsp. saffron threads or food coloring
½ tsp. sweet paprika
salt to taste
Spanish extra virgin olive oil

1. Soak the clams in a large bowl with water for 1 hour to get rid of the sand. Change the water at least twice.
2. Use a paella pan (paellera) which is a large flat open round pan with handles or a large electric skillet or pan with a base at least 40 cm. (15-16 inches) wide.
3. Heat 4 lugs of oil and fry the shrimps and Norway Lobsters over a medium heat until they're pink on both sides. Season with salt. Take them out of the paellera. Set aside.
4. Finely chop the garlic cloves and fry for 1 minute and then stir in the finely chopped green pepper and onion. Fry until they're tender.
5. Mix in the squid rings and fry for 3 minutes. Add in the tomato and combine. Season with the sweet paprika and salt. Over a medium-low heat, gently cook the mixture in the centre of the paellera with the lid on, stirring frequently for 5 minutes.
6. Add the rice to the paellera and cook for 5-7 minutes over a medium heat, stirring constantly.
7. Pour in the seafood stock and frozen peas. You can buy the stock already made or prepare it yourself. To make stock, follow the recipe on page 78.
8. Increase the heat to high. From this point on, do not stir or disturb the rice. Just move the paellera around to even out the heat. Bring to a boil and then adjust the heat to maintain a vigorous simmer until the rice appears at the level of the stock, about 10 minutes.
9. Put the saffron threads into a mortar and crush them into dust. Pour 1 Tbsp. of broth from the Paella into the mortar. Mix it with the saffron dust and stir well. Pour the resulting orange liquid into the paellera. If you can't find saffron, you can use 1 tsp. of orange coloring directly into the Paella.
10. Take the clams out of the bowl and rinse them under cold water. Add in the mussels and clams. Put on a lid and lower the heat so it simmers for about 5 more minutes.
11. Arrange the shrimps and Norway lobsters in the paellera, pushing them into the rice. Continue simmering covered until the liquid is absorbed and the rice is tender but still firm (about 5 more minutes). If the fish stock seems to be evaporating too quickly, add a little more stock or water. If the mussels or clams are still undercooked by the time the rice is done, cover loosely with foil for a few minutes to trap the heat and finish the cooking.
12. The rice should be tender but firm. Once cooked, remove the Paella from the heat and cover with a damp cloth and let it stand for about 5 minutes. The crunchy crust rice that sticks to the bottom of the paellera is the reward for a well-made Paella and is called "Socarrat". It's a real delicacy!

RICE ON THE SIDE Arroz a banda

Valencian fishermen invented this recipe when they went out at sea on their fishing boats. The rice was traditionally served on the side of the plate with the seafood and fish that was used to make the fish stock. Nowadays, some cooks use onion and garlic to prepare it but here I'll show you the authentic traditional recipe.

SERVES 4
400 gr. (13 oz.) bomb or round rice
200 gr. (6 oz.) cuttlefish, diced
1 large peeled tomato, diced
1 liter (4 cups) fish stock (on page 78)
500 raw shrimps/prawns, unpeeled
1/2 tsp. saffron threads or food coloring for paella
½ tsp. sweet paprika
salt to taste
Spanish extra virgin olive oil
aioli (optional) recipe on page 79

1. In a paellera pan, as described in the other Paella recipes, heat 3 lugs of olive oil and fry the cuttlefish dices until golden over a medium heat. Stir in the shrimps and fry until pink on both sides.
2. Stir in the diced tomato and combine with the rest of ingredients. Fry, stirring constantly for 5 minutes.
3. Add the rice to the paellera and cook for 5-7 minutes over a medium heat, stirring constantly.
4. Pour in 1 liter of fish stock (see recipe on page 78). Season with salt.
5. Put the saffron threads into a mortar and crush them into dust. Pour 1 Tbsp. of broth from the Paella into the mortar. Mix it with the saffron dust and stir well. Pour the resulting orange liquid into the paellera. If you can't find saffron, you can use 1 tsp. of orange coloring directly into the Paella.
6. Increase the heat to high. From this point on, do not stir or disturb the rice. Just move the paellera around to even out the heat. Bring to a boil and then lower the heat to maintain a simmer for about 15-18 minutes from the moment when the stock was added.
7. The rice should be tender but firm. Once cooked, remove the Paella from the heat and cover with a damp cloth and let it stand for about 5 minutes. It is usually served with a spoonful of aioli (recipe on page 79).

CUBAN STYLE RICE Arroz a la Cubana

Despite the name, this is a traditional dish in Spain's gastronomy, especially in the Canary Islands. It was created by the Spanish "emigrés" in South and Central America during colonial times. The popular Latin-American version has a fried banana in it, but it didn't really catch on in Spain.

SERVES 1: 1 egg - 50 gr. (1.7 oz.) rice - 30 ml. (2 Tbsp.) fried tomato puree - olive oil – salt to taste - parsley

1. Boil the rice according to the manufacturer's instructions. Drain and set aside.
2. Crack one egg onto a plate and season with salt.
3. Heat up 2 Tbsp. olive oil in a small pan over a medium-high heat. Carefully slip the egg into the oil and immediately turn the heat down to low. Fry until edges of the egg whites are golden. Tilt the frying pan and pour oil from the pan over the egg with a ladle or spoon, in order to also fry the top. But don't pour hot olive oil over the egg yolk if you like a runny yolk
4. Warm up the fried tomato puree in the microwave with a lid on for 15 seconds or in a pot over a low heat.
5. Place the fried egg with the boiled rice on a plate. Pour the tomato puree all over the rice and decorate with parsley.

TIP: Try it with canned tuna in olive oil. Drain and flake with a fork and sprinkle it all over the plate. Delicious!

BLACK RICE Arroz negro

The origins of this recipe are unknown, but it's a fact that squid ink has been used in Spanish Gastronomy since the 18ᵗʰ century. This is considered one of the most exclusive rice dishes in the whole of Spain.

SERVES 4
400 gr. (13 oz.) bomb or round rice
300 gr. (6 oz.) clean cuttlefish or squid, diced or in rings
1 large peeled tomato, grated
3 little packets of squid ink (16 gr./0.56 oz. each)
1 liter (4 cups) fish stock (see page 78)
2 garlic cloves, finely minced
200 gr. (7 oz.) raw shrimps/prawns, peeled
1/2 tsp. saffron threads
½ tsp. sweet paprika
salt to taste
Spanish extra virgin olive oil
aioli recipe on page 79

1. In a paellera pan, as described in the other Paella recipes, heat 2 Tbsp. of olive oil and fry the garlic over a medium heat for 30 seconds.
2. Stir in and fry the squid dices until golden over a medium-high heat. Stir constantly.
3. Cut the peeled tomato in half and grate. Stir it in the paellera with the garlic and squid and combine. Fry for 5 minutes. Pour in some more oil if you see the pan is getting a bit dry.
4. Put the saffron threads and paprika into a mortar and crush them into dust. Pour 1 Tbsp. of water into the mortar. Mix it with the saffron dust and paprika and stir well. Pour the resulting orange liquid into the paellera. Combine.
5. Add the rice and salt to taste to the paellera. Combine well and cook for about 5 minutes over a medium heat, stirring constantly.
6. Pour in 1 liter (4 cups) of fish stock (recipe on page 78) and squid ink. Combine well and increase the heat to high. From this point on, do not stir or disturb the rice. Just move the paellera around to even out the heat. Bring to a boil and then, after 4 minutes, lower the heat to maintain a simmer for about 10 minutes more. Stir in the peeled prawns, pushing them into the rice and simmer with a lid on for 5 minutes.
7. The rice should be tender but firm. Once cooked, remove the Paella from the heat and cover with a damp cloth to let it stand for about 5 minutes. It is usually served with a spoonful of aioli (recipe on page79).

POTATOES WITH RICE Patatas con arroz

This recipe is not very well known abroad. Here I'll let you in on a secret that a few Spaniards know about. It's unusual because it's a rice recipe eaten with a spoon.

SERVES 4 -6
400 gr. (1 ¼ cup) round rice
750 gr. (1.5 lb.) potatoes
2 garlic cloves
½ tsp. sweet paprika
1 bay leaf
1 ½ liter (6 cups) water
salt to taste
Spanish extra virgin olive oil

1. Fry one finely minced garlic clove in a pan with 2 Tbsp. of olive oil over a medium heat until light golden. Remove the pan from the heat and sprinkle the sweet paprika over the pan. Set aside.
2. Peel the potatoes and cut into middle size chunks. Heat up salted water with 1 crushed garlic clove and 1 bay leaf in a large sauce pan. There must be at least enough water to cover the potatoes. Pour in the contents of the frying pan. Bring to a boil and stir in the potatoes. Simmer covered over a medium-low heat for 10 minutes. Add in the rice and simmer for 15-20 minutes. Try and adjust salt. Let it rest for 5 minutes. The rice shouldn't be dry. It should have a soupy consistency. If the water seems to be evaporating too quickly while you are cooking the rice, then add a drop more.

MEAT

PORK WITH RED PEPPERS (40)

TOLEDO STYLE RABBIT (40)

BEEF STEW WITH FUNGHI-FRICANDÓ (41)

VEAL STEW (41)

BEEF TENDERLOINS WITH WINE (42)

BATTERED SANDWICH BEEF (42)

GUADALAJARA CHICKEN IN ALMOND SAUCE (43)

CHILINDRON CHICKEN (43)

ROAST CHICKEN WITH HERBS (44)

QUAILS SEGOVIA STYLE (44)

SPANISH ROAST LAMB (45)

LAMB CHOPS WITH PEPPERS (45)

Pork with red peppers

Toledo style rabbit

Beef stew with funghi

Guadalajara chicken in almond sauce

Roast chicken with herbs

Chilindron chicken

Lamb chops with peppers

Quails Segovia style

Veal stew

Battered sandwich beef

Spanish roast lamb

PORK WITH RED PEPPERS
Cerdo con pimientos rojos

A delicious recipe which can be served either with roast, fried or mashed potatoes. It's very Spanish, very typical and very easy. This recipe originally comes from Navarra, whose red peppers (and many other vegetables like asparagus) are very well known for their extraordinary quality and flavor. Don't use hot peppers as they will ruin the recipe. One more thing: don't forget to get a nice loaf of crusty bread to dip in the sauce.

SERVES 3-4
8 Pork loins
2 peeled garlic cloves, finely chopped
1 onion, finely chopped
2 red bell peppers
2 small potatoes
250 ml. (1 cup) fried tomato puree
125 ml. (1/2 cup) milk
125 ml. (1/2 cup) glass of red wine
salt to taste
Spanish extra virgin olive oil
a handful of ground chives for decoration

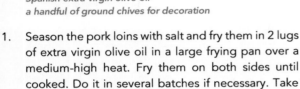

1. Season the pork loins with salt and fry them in 2 lugs of extra virgin olive oil in a large frying pan over a medium-high heat. Fry them on both sides until cooked. Do it in several batches if necessary. Take them out of the pan and set aside on a plate.
2. Wash and peel the peppers with a carrot peeler. Cut them into stripes.
3. Fry the pepper stripes, garlic and onion in the same olive oil where you fried the loins. Season with salt to taste. You can cover the pan with a lid to speed up the process.
4. When the vegetables are tender, pour the fried tomato puree into the pan and mix well.
5. Pour in the milk and wine and combine. Place the fried pork loins back in the pan and push them down to the bottom so they are covered by the sauce. Cook uncovered for 5 minutes. Then put on the lid and simmer over a medium-low heat for 15 minutes.
6. Cook the potatoes following the recipe on page 80 or fry them.
7. Spoon the potato cubes into the pan and mix well. Simmer covered for 5 minutes. Right before serving, sprinkle ground parsley all over the ingredients. You can decorate with chives.

TOLEDO STYLE RABBIT
Conejo a la Toledana

This traditional dish is eaten all year round as a first course. It can be accompanied by roast potatoes, mash potatoes or rice if you want to turn it into a main course. You can also make it with hare, but you would have to cook it for an extra half an hour.

SERVES 4
1 kg. (2.2 lb.) rabbit cut into pieces
2 onions
2 unpeeled garlic cloves
3 carrots
½ glass wine vinegar
1 glass white wine
12 stuffed green olives
1 bay leaf
5 peppercorns
6 thyme branches
salt to taste
ground black pepper
60 ml. (2 fl. oz.) Spanish extra virgin olive oil

1. Season the rabbit pieces with salt and ground pepper and fry in a wide casserole with the oil until golden outside. Remove the pieces and set aside on a plate.
2. Peel and finely mince the onions. Peel, wash and cut the carrots into thin slices. Place the onions and carrots in the oil left over from frying the rabbit. Fry over a medium heat. When they begin to soften, add the thyme, bay leaf, unpeeled garlic cloves, peppercorns and rabbit pieces.
3. Fry for 5 minutes.
4. Add the vinegar, white wine and a pinch of salt and cover with water.
5. Bring to a boil, then lower the heat to medium-low, cover with a lid and simmer for about 1 hour. The time depends on the age and size of the rabbit. Cook until the rabbit is tender. Add the green olives into the saucepan 10 minutes before you finish cooking the rabbit.
6. Serve immediately.

BEEF STEW WITH FUNGHI Fricandó

This is a traditional dish from the Catalonia Region. The first references to fricandó appear as early as the 18th century in some cooking books written by priests. It was usually made with "moixernós" mushrooms, but nowadays it can be found with any type of funghi.

SERVES 4
½ kg. (1 lb.) beef brisket in chunks
300 gr. (10 oz.) funghi
1 onion
1 tomato
125 ml. (1/2 cup) of brandy
50 gr. (1.7 oz.) flour
Spanish extra virgin olive oil
a handful of ground parsley for decoration
salt to taste
ground black pepper to taste

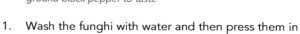

1. Wash the funghi with water and then press them in your hands to get rid of the excess water.
2. Cut the beef into regular size chunks about 1 inch. (2.5 cm) wide. Season with salt and black pepper. Coat each chunk in flour.
3. Heat up 3 lugs of oil in a casserole. When the oil is hot, fry the beef chunks over a medium-high heat until golden all over. Take the meat out of the casserole and set aside.
4. Lower the heat to medium. Add the finely chopped onion and diced peeled tomato. Fry them, stirring frequently until tender.
5. Add in the clean funghi and fry for 3 minutes stirring frequently.
6. Season with salt and pour in the brandy. Let the alcohol evaporate (cook uncovered for 6 minutes).
7. Pour in 500 ml. (2 cups) of water and spoon the beef chunks into the casserole. Bring to a boil over a high heat and then simmer covered with a lid over a lower heat for 1 hour until the meat is tender. If you want to reduce cooking times, you can use smaller beef chunks.

VEAL STEW Estofado de ternera

It's very important to get top quality meat as it must be simmered in white wine until tender. I usually buy a brisket in one piece and cut it myself into chunks the size I want. You can also buy the meat pre-cut into chunks. The best thing about this dish is that it keeps very well in the fridge, so you can prepare it one day ahead and the next day it will taste even better.

SERVES 4
1 Kg. (2.2 lb.) veal brisket in chunks
1 medium onion
3 medium carrots
1 glass of white wine
2 medium potatoes
80 gr. (3 oz.) frozen peas
2 bay leaves
1 Tbsp ground oregano
salt to taste
ground black pepper to taste
Spanish extra virgin olive oil

1. Heat 3 Tbsp. of olive oil in a large pot over a medium-high heat. Add in 2 bay leaves.
2. Cut the veal into regular size chunks about 1 inch. (2.5 cm.) wide. Season with salt and black pepper. When the oil is hot, add the finely chopped onion and veal chunks. Lower the heat to medium and fry them, stirring frequently until meat is medium brown on the outside and the onion is translucent. Pour in the wine and boil over a moderately high heat until almost evaporated (about 6 minutes).
3. Wash, peel and slice the carrots. Stir them into the pot. Cover with a lid and simmer over a low heat for 1 h 30 min until the meat is very tender (you could cut it with a fork). Stir and mix every now and then.
4. Stir in the frozen peas. Season with a pinch of salt and with ground oregano. Simmer covered for another 20 minutes.
5. Follow the potatoes recipe on page 80.
6. Spoon the potatoes into the pan and stir well. Cover and simmer for 15 minutes.
7. There you have it. The meat should be tender so it almost melts in your mouth. If it doesn't, simmer for as long as necessary. If you want to reduce cooking times, you can use smaller veal chunks.

BEEF TENDERLOINS WITH RED WINE   Solomillo al vino tinto

This traditional dish comes from La Rioja, whose still red wines are world famous. The harvesting of wine dates back to the Phoenicians and Celtiberians. Roman objects used for wine production have been found in La Rioja.

SERVES 6
6 beef tenderloins of 200 gr. (7 oz.) each
500 ml. (2 cups) Rioja still red wine
2 bay leaves
a bunch of fresh thyme
125 ml. (1/2 cup) cognac
200 ml. (3/4 cup) meat/chicken stock
12 pickled onions
12 mushrooms, sliced
1 Tbsp. flour
salt to taste
black ground pepper to taste
parsley
Spanish extra virgin olive oil

1. Macerate the tenderloins with the wine, bay leaves and thyme for 4-5 hours.
2. Fry the mushrooms in a pan with olive oil over medium-high heat and set aside.
3. Take the tenderloins out of the wine and place them on a plate. Season with salt and black ground pepper. Drain the wine to get rid of the bay leaves and thyme and set aside.
4. Heat 2 Tbsp. of olive oil in a large saucepan over a medium-high heat and fry the beef for one minute on each side. Take out and set aside covering in tin foil.
5. Fry 1 Tbsp. of flour in the remaining oil in the pan for 2 minutes over a medium heat If it's too dry, you can add a drizzle of oil.
6. Pour the cognac into the same sauce pan and flambé.
7. Pour in the drained red wine into the pan and let it reduce till half.
8. Stir in the beef stock, pickled onions and mushrooms.
9. Season with salt and pepper and simmer for about 15 minutes.
10. Place every tenderloin on a plate and cover with the sauce from the pan. Sprinkle with ground parsley on top.

BATTERED SANDWICH BEEF   Cachopo

This dish is one of signature dishes of Asturias. The original recipes consists of two steaks sandwiched together with cheese and cured ham but there are several variations which add mushrooms, bacon, red peppers, etc. There are major contests in Asturias between restaurants to see who makes the best "cachopo". Accompany with Asturian Cider for perfection.

SERVES 1
2 thin beef fillets
1 cured ham slice
2 cheese slices (cheddar, edam or similar)
Spanish extra virgin olive oil

For the Batter:
small plate of flour
small plate of breadcrumbs
1 beaten egg
salt to taste

1. Cover the fillets with cling film and pound them using a kitchen hammer. Remove the cling film and season each side evenly with salt. Place the cured ham and cheese slices between the 2 fillets, especially pressing the fillet edges to seal.
2. Prepare 3 plates: one with flour, another with beaten egg and the last one with breadcrumbs.
3. Cover your hands with flour. Lay the beef sandwich in the flour. Cover both sides, shaking off any excess.
4. Dip the beef sandwich in the beaten egg and coat both sides. Remove from the egg and lay it in the breadcrumbs coating both sides evenly.
5. Heat up a good amount of olive oil in a frying pan over a high-medium heat. The amount of oil depends on the size of the pan. The oil must cover the bottom half of the sandwich beef and be quite hot at first. When it's hot (but before getting smoky hot) place it carefully in the oil. Lower the heat to a medium heat. Fry for about 3-5 minutes in total, turning them half way through until they are golden brown on both sides. Drain on a paper towel lined base and serve.

GUADALAJARA CHICKEN IN ALMOND SAUCE

Pollo con almendras de Guadalajara

This recipe's origins are in the Spanish province of Guadalajara. The almond sauce is very tasty. You can either use whole almonds without skin and grind them at home or buy them already ground. Careful! You won't be able to resist dipping your bread in this delicious sauce.

SERVES 4
1 chicken, cut into pieces
2 garlic cloves
1 slice of sandwich bread
Spanish extra virgin olive oil
salt to taste
80 gr. (3 oz.) almonds
2 large potatoes
2 bay leaves

1. Heat 2 Tbsp. of oil in a large saucepan over a medium heat. Place 2 bay leaves and the chicken pieces first skin-side up in the pan. Fry them on both sides until medium golden. On the inside the chicken will still be raw.
2. Pour chicken stock or just water into the pan enough to cover the bottom half of the chicken. Cover with a lid and simmer over a medium-low heat for 30 minutes turning the chicken pieces every now and then.
3. Heat 3 Tbsp. of olive oil in a small frying pan over a medium heat and fry 2 peeled garlic cloves until golden on both sides. Set aside. In the same olive oil, fry both sides of a slice of sandwich bread.
4. Now you have 2 options:
a. Using a mortar: Crush the almonds in a mortar until ground. Spoon in the fried garlic cloves and bread and crush them with the pestle until you get a thick paste. Pour in 2 Tbsp of the chicken broth from the saucepan into the mortar and mix with the pestle.
b. Place the almonds, fried garlic, bread and 125 ml. (1/2 cup) of the chicken broth from the pan into a blender and blend until smooth. If you don't have enough broth in the pan, you can complete it with just water.
5. Pour the mixture into the saucepan and season with salt. Stir well. Simmer covered for 20 minutes or until the meat separates from the bone.
6. Follow the potatoes recipe on page 80.
7. Combine the potatoes with the chicken in the saucepan and simmer for 5 minutes. If the almond sauce gets too thick or too dry, you can add chicken stock or water.

CHILINDRON CHICKEN

Pollo al Chilindrón

This recipe comes from the Aragón region. Some say that the term "Chilindrón" comes from the olden Aragonese superlative word for big pepper. Others say this dish is named after a popular Aragonese card game. It's very traditional also in the Navarran region, but they don't usually use tomatoes. Try both and decide which version you prefer.

SERVES 4
1 chicken, cut into pieces
2 garlic cloves, finely minced
1 red bell pepper, diced
1 green bell pepper, diced
1 large onion, diced
4 ripe tomatoes, peeled
250 ml (1 cup). white wine
½ Tbsp. sweet paprika
1 bay leaf
Spanish extra virgin olive oil
ground black pepper to taste
salt to taste

1. Season the chicken pieces with salt and ground black pepper.
2. Heat 2 Tbsp. of olive oil in a large saucepan over a medium heat. Place 2 bay leaves and the chicken pieces first skin-side up in the pan. Fry them on both sides until medium golden. On the inside the chicken will still be raw. Take the chicken out of the pan and set aside on a plate.
3. Pour a bit more oil into the same pan and add the onion and peppers diced. Cook over a low heat, stirring occasionally for about 30 minutes.
4. Stir in the garlic cloves and cook for 5 minutes.
5. Place the chicken pieces back into the pan.
6. Cut the peeled tomatoes in half and grate. Stir them in and combine. Fry for 5 minutes.
7. Sprinkle sweet paprika all over.
8. Pour in ½ liter (2 cups) of water.
9. Simmer covered with a lid over a low heat for 1 hour or until the meat separates from the bone. You can serve it on its own or with mashed potato on the side.

ROAST CHICKEN WITH HERBS Pollo asado con hierbas

This recipe is eaten all over Spain. The quality of the chicken is rather important. I try to go for free range corn fed chicken since it's very tasty.

SERVES 4
4 large chicken legs with skin
Spanish extra virgin olive oil
salt to taste
4 bay leaves
1 Tbsp. oregano
1 Tbsp. thyme
1 Tbsp. parsley
1 Kg. potatoes
aioli (optional) recipe on page 79

1. Pre-heat oven to 390°F (200°C).
2. Peel and cut the potatoes into 0,8 cm (1/3 inch) wide slices or into irregular chunks. Place them on a baking tray and pour olive oil all over the slices. Combine the oil and potatoes with your hands.
3. Season the chicken with salt and all the herbs on both sides of the legs. Place them on the potatoes, skin up.
4. Pour the olive oil generously all over the chicken and massage the legs with your hands.
5. Roast the chicken legs and potatoes in the middle rack of the oven for about 20 minutes or until you see the skin is medium golden.
6. Turn the chicken pieces and roast again until that side is also medium golden (about 20 minutes).
7. Lower the heat to 175°C (350 °F) and cook for 30 minutes. Serve immediately.

TIP:You can serve it with aioli (recipe on page 80).

QUAILS SEGOVIA STYLE Perdices a la Segoviana

It may sound a little bit eccentric the fact you can find chocolate among the ingredients, but the truth is that it goes perfectly with the quails and rest of the ingredients. It is exquisite.

SERVES 4
4 quails, cleaned (ask your butcher to do it for you)
2 carrots, sliced
1 medium onion, minced
1 tomato, peeled and grated
1 garlic clove, finely minced
8 mushrooms, sliced
ground black pepper
butter
1 Tbsp. flour

250 ml. (1 cup) chicken stock
125 ml. (1/2 cup) white wine
60 ml. (1/4 cup) sherry
1 Tbsp. of grated dark chocolate
salt to taste
Spanish extra virgin olive oil
1 bay leaf
1 Tbsp. oregano
1 Tbsp. thyme
1 Tbsp. parsley

1. Season quails with salt and pepper. Rub the skin with a bit of butter.
2. Sprinkle salt, oregano and thyme over the quails.
3. Heat 3 Tbsp.of oil in a large saucepan over a medium-high heat. Place 1 bay leaf and the quails in the pan. Fry turning them until medium golden completely on the outside. On the inside the quails will still be raw. Take the quails out and set aside on a plate.
4. In the same oil, fry the garlic, onion and carrots over a medium-low heat until tender. After 5 minutes, stir in the sliced mushrooms. Cook until soft. Add in the flour and cook for 1 minute.
5. Stir in the tomato and fry for 2 minutes.
6. Place the quails back into the pan. Pour in the stock, white wine and sherry. Stir in the grated chocolate. Cook for about 30 minutes covered until quails are tender over a medium heat, turning them every now and then. Sprinkle with parsley before serving.

TIP: Serve with boiled rice

SPANISH ROAST LAMB Asado de cordero

This is a very traditional recipe in the region of Aragón. It's a must on Christmas day and on special occasions. In some parts of Spain like Catalonia, it is accompanied with aioli, which is a sort of garlic mayonnaise. The lamb traditionally used in Aragón is "ternasco lechal" which is a 30 to 45 days old lamb which has been suckled or fed only on milk. You can imagine how tender and exquisite the meat is. If you ever visit Aragón, don't miss the opportunity to try it.

SERVES 4
1 leg or shoulder of top quality lamb, weighing about 1.5 kg. (3.3 lb.)
Spanish extra virgin olive oil
salt to taste
wine vinegar
(1 kg./2.2 lb.) potatoes
2 garlic cloves
aioli (see recipe page 79)

1. Line a baking tray with baking paper. Place the lamb on it. Cut the leg of lamb into individual portions. If you prefer, your butcher can cut it for you.
2. Rub 2 peeled garlic cloves all over the lamb. Season with salt to taste and then drizzle 3 Tbsp. of olive oil over the lamb. Let stand at room temperature for 1 hour.
3. Pre-heat oven to 220°C (420°F).
4. You will first need to roast the lamb in the oven at a high temperature and slightly brown the outside to seal the meat. This will keep in the juices for when you slowly cook it afterwards. Start by roasting the lamb in the middle rack of the oven at 220°C (420°F). When you see it brown on the outside (about 10-15 minutes), place the potatoes around the lamb. Turn the meat pieces and roast again until that side is also golden brown (about 10 minutes).
5. Peel and cut the potatoes into 0,8 cm (1/3 inch) wide slices. Season with salt. Place them on the baking tray around the meat and pour olive oil all over the slices.
6. Then, lower the temperature to 165°C (330°F) and cook for around 30 minutes.
7. When there's only 20 minutes left to roast, brush the lamb with wine vinegar. When the lamb is cooked, turn off the heat and leave inside the oven for a further 5 minutes. Serve immediately with or without aioli (preparation steps are on page 79).

LAMB CHOPS WITH PEPPERS   Chuletas de cordero con pimientos

This traditional dish is very popular in the Extremadura region.

SERVES 4
8-10 leg lamb chops
1 onion
1 red bell pepper
1 green bell pepper
1 bay leaf
125 ml. (1/2 cup) white wine
45 ml. (3 Tbsp.) Spanish extra virgin olive oil
salt to taste

1. Season the lamb chops with salt and fry in a wide casserole with oil until golden outside. Remove the pieces and set aside on a plate.
2. Peel and finely mince the onion. Peel, wash and cut the peppers into strips. Place the onions and peppers in the oil left over from frying the lamb. Fry over a medium heat. Season with salt. When they begin to soften, add the white wine and bay leaf. Bring to a boil and cook for about 5 minutes over a medium-high heat until the alcohol smell fades, meaning that the alcohol has evaporated.
3. Place the lamb chops back into the pan. Combine, cover with a lid and simmer for 10 minutes over a low heat.

FISH

PAPRIKA & GARLIC MONKFISH (48)

ORIO SEA BREAM (48)

FRESH TUNA STEW (49)

PAN GRILLED SWORDFISH (49)

SARDINES IN ONION SAUCE (50)

FRIED FISH (50)

ANCHOVIES MARINATED IN VINEGAR (50)

OVEN BAKED SALMON (51)

NAVARRAN TROUT (51)

COD STUFFED "PIQUILLO" RED PEPPERS (52)

HAKE IN GREEN SAUCE (52)

FISH STEW (53)

COD WITH ONION (53)

Paprika & garlic monkfish

Pan grilled swordfish

Sardines in onion sauce

Orio sea bream

Oven baked salmon

Fresh tuna stew

Marinated anchovies in vinegar

Fried fish

Hake in green sauce

Cod stuffed red peppers

Navarran trout

PAPRIKA & GARLIC MONKFISH All i pebre

This recipe comes from Valencia and was originally made using eels. Now, in addition to eels, there are different versions, the most popular one being with monkfish, as shown in this recipe. The name of the recipe refers to the sauce whose basic ingredients are garlic and sweet paprika.

SERVES 4
4 monkfish tails
1/2 tsp. sweet paprika
1 bay leaf
4 garlic cloves
2 large potatoes
75 gr. (2.6 oz.) skinned almonds
125 ml. (1/2 cup) fish stock
45 ml. (3 Tbsp.) Spanish extra virgin olive oil
salt to taste

1. Heat the oil in a large pan and fry 4 unpeeled garlic cloves over a medium-low heat until golden on both sides. Be careful not to brown them. Take out of the pan and let cool for 5 minutes. Peel them with your hands and crush them in a mortar. Add the almonds in the mortar and crush well. If you don't have a mortar, you can use a grinder. Set aside.
2. Peel and wash the potatoes. Cut into slices and wash again. Dry them with a paper towel. Fry them until golden, over a medium heat in the same oil where you fried the garlic. Salt to taste. Take them out with a slotted spoon and set aside on a plate.
3. Season the monkfish tails with salt and fry them on both sides until golden.
4. Add the fried potatoes that you had set aside. Sprinkle the paprika on the ingredients in the pan and fry for 3 minutes. Be careful no to burn the paprika.
5. Pour the mortar mixture into the pan. Add the fish stock (recipe on page 78) until the bottom half of the fish is covered. Add the bay leaf and boil for 10 minutes, turning the fish over half way through.
6. The stock should have thickened and reduced so you have a nice sauce.

ORIO SEA BREAM Dorada al Orio

This recipe originally comes from the town of Orio in the Basque Country and can be made with different types of fish like flounder or hake. Northern Spain is very well-known for its fish recipes and this one is very popular among Spaniards.

SERVES 4
8 clean sea bream fillets
4 garlic cloves
3 potatoes
squeeze of lemon juice
Spanish extra virgin olive oil
salt to taste

1. Pre-heat oven to 200°C (392°F).
2. Line an oven tray with baking paper. Pour a little olive oil on the paper and then place the fish skin-side down. Move it around with your hands to spread the olive oil all over the paper. Season with salt. Cook in oven for 10 minutes.
3. Meanwhile, cut the potatoes into chunks (2.5cm /1 inch) and cook them following recipe on page 80.
4. Heat 3-4 Tbsp. of olive oil in a small frying pan over a medium heat. Fry the finely chopped garlic cloves until light golden. Be careful because they can get burnt really quickly.
5. Turn off the heat and remove the pan. Let it cool for 2 minutes. The oil will keep on cooking the garlic even though the pan is off the heat. At that moment, when the oil is not too hot, add a squeeze of lemon juice.
6. Take the tray out of the oven and place the potatoes around the fish. Spoon the garlic oil over the fillets. Cook in the oven for a further 5-10 minutes at 180°C (350°F).
7. Serve immediately and enjoy.

FRESH TUNA STEW Marmitako

Marmitako means "from the pot" in Basque, marmita meaning pot in Basque. This is one of the icon dishes of the Basque Country gastronomy. It's a traditional fisherman's meal which they used to prepare on their fishing boats when they were out at sea. It's a bit difficult to find one of its main ingredients called "pimiento choricero" which is a type of dried red pepper with a very particular flavor. Sometimes you can find it outside Spain in a jar that says "carne de pimiento chorizo" which is the pulp of the pepper. Try a delicatessen near you or an import online store which sells Spanish products. If the worse comes to worst, you can always make the recipe without it.

SERVES 4
4 Potatoes, peeled
500 gr. (17 oz.) skinless fresh tuna
2 chives, diced
2 small green peppers, diced
1 garlic head
4 "choricero peppers"
250 ml. (1 cup) fried tomato sauce

1 slice of sandwich toast
125 ml. (1/2 cup) white wine or brandy
Spanish extra virgin olive oil
ground black pepper to taste
1 small cayenne pepper
salt to taste
a handful of parsley

1. Take off the stems and seeds of the choricero peppers. Soak them in a small bowl with hot water until they are tender (around 20 minutes). Then scrape off of with a blunt knife the inner pulp. Set aside.
2. Cut the potatoes into chunks (1 inch/ 2.5 cm wide). Boil them for 20 minutes in a pot with water, the whole garlic head, the brandy or white wine and the cayenne pepper.
3. Meanwhile, in a casserole, heat 4 Tbsp. olive oil. Add in the green peppers and chives. Season with salt. Fry over medium-low heat, stirring frequently until tender.
4. Spoon the pulp of the choricero peppers and tomato sauce into the casserole and combine well with the vegetables. Take off the heat.
5. When the potatoes have been boiling for 20 minutes, pour the contents of the casserole with the vegetables into the pot with the water and potatoes. Combine.
6. Break up the sandwich toast with your hands and add into the pot. Cook for 10 minutes over a medium heat.
7. Cut the tuna into chunks (2.5 cm. /1 inch wide). Season the fresh tuna with salt and black pepper.
8. Turn off the heat and add the tuna in the pot. Sprinkle with parsley.
9. Wait for 3 minutes and serve warm.

TIP: Try this recipe with any type of fish.

PAN GRILLED SWORDFISH Emperador a la plancha

This is the ideal way to prepare this type of fish because by grilling it, the fish will be crispy on the outside but tender on the inside.

SERVES 4
4 swordfish fillets
2 large garlic cloves
a handful of parsley
a squeeze of lemon juice
lemon wedges to decorate
Spanish extra virgin olive oil
salt to taste

1. Peel the garlic cloves and crush in a mortar. Add the parsley and a pinch of salt. Continue crushing until you get an homogeneous paste. Pour 50 ml. (3 Tbsp.) of olive oil into the mortar slowly while stirring the paste with the pestle. Pour in a squeeze of fresh lemon juice at the end. If you haven't got a mortar, you can use a hand blender
2. Season the fillets with salt. Heat 1 Tbsp.of oil in a large non-stickpan and when hot, grill the fillets for about 3 minutes on each side. Place each fillet on a plate.
3. Spoon the garlic sauce over the fish and serve immediately.

SARDINES IN ONION SAUCE

Sardinas encebolladas

This dish is very well known in Northern Spain. The secret is to slowly cook the sardines with the onion. It is very important to get good quality fish. You can also use other types of blue fish like mackerel, mullet etc.

SERVES 4
500 gr. (1.7 oz.) sardines, scaled, gutted and headless
30 ml. (2 Tbsp.) Spanish extra virgin olive oil
1 ½ Tbsp. white wine vinegar
1 large onion
3 bay leaves
salt to taste

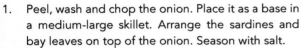

1. Peel, wash and chop the onion. Place it as a base in a medium-large skillet. Arrange the sardines and bay leaves on top of the onion. Season with salt.
2. Pour 3 lugs of oil all over the ingredients. Heat the skillet over a medium heat and when you see that the onion starts to fry, lower the heat to low. Cover with a lid and let it simmer.
3. Check it after 10 minutes and see how the onion starts exuding liquid from within. Continue simmering in the onion liquid with a lid on. After about 30 minutes, the liquid will have reduced considerably but the onion will still be white. Then pour the vinegar all over the ingredients. Cover again with a lid and simmer until the liquid has reduced almost completely and the onion is golden brown (about 15 more minutes). Serve immediately.

FRIED FISH Pescaíto Frito

Here we deep fry small fresh fish in very hot olive oil for a few seconds. It's very typical in Andalusia, but you can also find it along the rest of the Mediterranean Coast. Anchovies are mainly used, but an assortment of different types of small fish are very common as well, like red mullets, dogfish and whitebait. Anchovies are usually gutted, scaled and headless but if the fish is very small, like whitebait, you don't need to clean the fish as it is eaten whole with bones and heads.

SERVES 4:
1 kg. (2.2 lb.) good quality fresh anchovies, scaled, gutted and headless or any other small fish
flour
Spanish extra virgin olive oil
salt to taste

1. Season the fish with salt. Place the flour in a bowl or plate. Make sure the fish is dry and coat it with the flour, shaking off any excess.
2. Heat up a good amount of olive oil in a small frying pan or pot. The best is to fry the fish in batches since the oil should cover them completely. When it's hot (180°C/356°F), place the fish into the pan and fry over a high-medium heat. Fry for 40 seconds, if you use very small fish like whitebait or very small anchovies. Fry for around 2 minutes, if you use larger fish.
3. Using a slotted spoon, lift out the fish, holding them briefly over the pan to allow the excess oil to drain. Transfer to a plate lined with kitchen roll to drain further. Serve immediately.

ANCHOVIES MARINATED IN VINEGAR

Boquerones en Vinagre

This recipe's origins are is in Andalusia but you can find it all over Spain. Deep-freeze the fresh anchovies for at least 4 days to avoid anisakis. Just unthaw them before starting the recipe. The marinade will sort of cure the fish, which will allow it to keep up to 1 week in the fridge.

SERVES 4:
1 kg. (2.2 lb.) good quality fresh anchovies, scaled, gutted and headless
300 ml. (1 ¼ cup) white wine vinegar
4 garlic cloves
a handful of fresh parsley
Spanish extra virgin olive oil
salt to taste

1. Mix the vinegar with 125 ml. (1/2 cup) cold water in a deep square glass dish similar to a Tupperware. Dip the fish, skin down in the marinade. Season with salt and combine with your hands. The marinade should cover the fish completely. Cover the dish with a lid or cling film. Leave in the fridge for 48 hours.
2. Take the fish out of the marinade and wash well under tap water. Dry with kitchen roll and transfer to a platter or plate. Mix the garlic, 60 ml. (4 Tbsp.) oil and a bunch of parsley in a bowl and spoon it over the fish. Let it rest covered with a lid or film for 2 hours in the fridge. After that time they fish will be ready to enjoy.

OVEN BAKED SALMON Salmón al horno

In Spain, there is still a lot of fishing of Wild Salmon on the banks of the rivers that flow into the Cantabric Sea and the Atlantic. Its fatty acids make this recipe a very healthy meal. Quick and easy to prepare, it is an ideal meal when you have little time or desire to cook. You can accompany the salmon with boiled rice and mayonnaise.

SERVES 4
4 salmon fillets
1 large tomato
1 tsp. sweet paprika
4 bay leaves
2 Tbsp. lemon juice
½ lemon, sliced
1 Tbsp. chopped basil
1 Tbsp. ground oregano
1 Tbsp. chopped thyme or 4 thyme branches
Spanish extra virgin olive oil
salt to taste

1. Pre-heat oven to 200°C (392°F).
2. Line an oven dish with baking paper and place the salmon fillets skin-side down.
3. Add in all the spices, salt, sliced tomato and sliced lemon.
4. Bake at 200°C (392°F) for 20 minutes or until cooked through. To check it, insert a fork into the salmon and gently twist. The salmon is done as soon as it begins to flake. Be sure to test at the minimum baking time. When done, the salmon will be opaque with milky-white juices. Don't over cook it or your fish will be dry.
5. Serve immediately pouring the juices from the tray all over the salmon. It will be delicious.

NAVARRAN TROUT Trucha a la Navarra

The Navarran Region is full of rivers and brooks so it's no wonder why among its best well known recipes include this one. It is so delicious that it is now very popular all over Spain. It is a celebration of flavors.

SERVES 2
2 trouts scaled, gutted and headless
4 cured ham slices
Spanish extra virgin olive oil
flour
lemon slices
salt to taste

1. Pre-heat oven to 180°C (355 °F).
2. Remove the bones with tweezers. Season the insides with salt. Place 2 cured ham slices between the loins of each trout.
3. Coat the trout slightly with flour on both sides. Top each trout with one lemon slice.
4. Place the fish in a deep baking tray. Drizzle with olive oil.
5. Roast on a middle rack for about 15 minutes.
6. Drizzle any juices leftover in the baking tray over the trouts before serving.

COD STUFFED "PIQUILLO" PEPPERS Pimientos del Piquillo rellenos de bacalao

The "Pimientos del Piquillo" are deep flavored roasted red peppers in oil and are the ones used in this recipe. Traditionally from Navarra in Spain, nowadays they can be bought in many countries. But if you can't find them, you can use any roasted red peppers. I just love them because they can be filled with practically any ingredient.

SERVES 4
500 gr. (17 oz.) fresh cod
150 gr. (5 oz.) peeled shrimps
1 onion
2 Tbsp. wheat flour
200 ml. (7 fl. oz.) milk
1 glass of white wine
2 Tbsp. fried tomato puree
salt to taste
ground black pepper

1 Tbsp. parsley
Spanish virgin olive oil
a handful of grated cheese
For the bechamel:
cold milk
oil, butter or margarine
wheat flour
1 tsp. of salt

1. Pre-heat the oven to 200°C (395°F). Wash the fish and press it in your hands so all the water in it comes out. Fry the fish in a medium-large frying pan with a splash of Spanish virgin olive oil over a medium heat. You can start mincing the fish with a wooden spatula. Once the fish is cooked through, remove from heat. I recommend you mince the fish with a food processor once it's cooked. Spoon the fish onto a plate.
2. In the same pan, pour in 2 tbsp. of olive oil and fry the finely chopped onion and chopped shrimps over a medium heat until tender (about 3 minutes). Mix in the cooked fish and 2 Tbsp. of wheat flour. After one minute, add the milk and glass of wine. After 5 minutes, pour in the fried tomato puree. Stir and cook for 3 minutes over a medium heat. Sprinkle parsley and grated cheese over the mixture and cook until it melts. It should be moist but not runny. Spoon onto a plate and let it cool for 15 minutes.
3. Fill the peppers carefully and lay them on their side in an oven-proof dish.
4. Prepare the classic bechamel following steps on page 79.
5. Cover the red peppers with the bechamel. Sprinkle grated cheese and grill in the oven until golden brown.

HAKE IN GREEN SAUCE Merluza en salsa verde.

This is an iconic recipe of the Basque Gastronomy with an iconic sauce used in many other Basque recipes.

SERVES 4
8 hake loins
3 garlic cloves, finely minced
2 Tbsp. of flour
150 gr. (5 oz.) frozen peas
125 ml. (1/2 cup) white wine
250 gr. (8.8 oz.) fresh clams
250 ml. (1 cup) fish stock (page 79)
a handful of fresh parsley, minced
Spanish extra virgin olive oil
salt to taste

1. Season the hake with salt. Soak the clams in a bowl with water and salt for 2 hours.
2. Heat 3 Tbsp. of olive oil in a large sauce pan and fry the garlic over medium heat for 1 minute. Then fry the flour, stirring constantly for 1 minute.
3. Pour in the wine and fish stock (enough so the liquid covers bottom half of the hake). Stir in the peas and season with a pinch of salt. Bring to a boil and cook with the lid off for 5 minutes over a medium heat
4. Place the fish into the pan and cook it covered for 3 minutes . Then, carefully turn every fish loin over. Drain the clams out of the bowl and stir into the pan. Sprinkle parsley and cook covered with a lid for another 3 minutes over a medium-low heat.

TIP: Add a few white/green asparagus or boiled eggs when you turn the loins in the pan.

FISH STEW Guisado de Pescado

This recipe is very typical and you can find very different varieties along the Mediterranean coast. It's a fishermen's dish they used to cook when they were out at sea. A real delicacy!. Cod is mainly used in this recipe but you can substitute it for any other white fish like monkfish, hake, etc.

SERVES 4
500 gr. (1.3 lb.) skinless and boneless fresh cod loins
12 raw peeled shrimps/prawns
6 raw unpeeled shrimps/prawns
1 small onion
½ green bell pepper
45 ml. (3 Tbsp.) fried tomato puree
1 bay leaf
2 garlic cloves
500 gr. (17 oz.) peeled potato in chunks
200 gr. (6 oz.) squid chunks or rings
Spanish extra virgin olive oil
salt to taste
70 gr. (2.5 oz.) dry short vermicelli noodles (optional)

1. Coat a large pan with 3 Tbsp. of olive oil. Season the shrimps (peeled and unpeeled) with salt and fry on both sides over a medium heat until pink. Take out of the pan and set aside.
2. Finely chop the green pepper, garlic and onion. Add them to the pan. Place the fish loins into the pan. Cook all these ingredients in the pan until vegetables are done.
3. Mix in the squid and bay leaf and cook for 3 min. Add a drizzle of oil if you see the pan gets too dry. Pour in the tomato puree and season with salt. Cook with a lid on for 5 min, stirring frequently.
4. Stir in the potato chunks and noodles (if using). Fry for about 5 min. over a medium heat, stirring constantly.
5. Add enough water to cover the potatoes and bring to a boil over medium heat. Cook covered for 8 min.
6. Then, take the lid off and cook until potatoes are tender. Keep an eye on the stew and if you see it starts to get too dry you can put the lid on and/or add more water. The stew should have a soupy consistency at the end. Try and adjust salt. Stir the shrimps set aside earlier into the pan 5 minutes before finishing cooking.

COD WITH ONION

Bacalao encebollado

This recipe is very easy and simple. The salty flavor of the cod combines very well with the sweetness of the slowly cooked onion and potatoes.

SERVES 4
500 gr. (1.3 lb.) skinless and boneless fresh cod loins
350 gr. (12 oz.) onions
750 gr. (1.7 lb.) potatoes
Spanish extra virgin olive oil
salt to taste
ground parsley

1. Peel and wash the onions and potatoes. Cut the onions into thin strips and the potatoes into thin half slices, just like you would for a Spanish Potato Omelette (recipe on page 22).
2. Heat 3 Tbsp. of olive oil in a large saucepan over a medium heat. When hot, fry the cod loins first skin-side up in the pan. Fry them for 1 minute on each side over a high-medium heat. On the inside the fish will be still a bit raw. Take the loins out of the pan and set aside on a plate.
3. Pour a bit more oil into the same pan if you see it's dry and add the onion and potatoes. Season with salt. Cook covered over a low heat, stirring occasionally until potatoes are tender (for about 20 minutes).
4. Place the cod loins on top, pushing them down into the potatoes and onions. Cook covered over a low heat until the fish is cooked thoroughly (around 5-7 minutes).
5. Sprinkle ground parsley on top.
6. You can flake the fish with a fork and stir it up with the rest of the ingredients before serving.

SEAFOOD

GRILLED CUTTLEFISH (56)

BATTERED SQUID (56)

GALICIAN STYLE OCTOPUS (57)

RAZOR CLAMS IN GARLIC SAUCE (57)

CLAMS IN GREEN SAUCE (58)

BOILED SEA SNAILS (58)

SHRIMP GARLIC STYLE "AL AJILLO" (59)

GRILLED PRAWNS (59)

STEAMED MUSSELS (59)

Battered squid

Shrimp garlic style

Galician style octopus

Clams in green sauce

Razor clams in garlic sauce

Grilled shrimps

Boiled sea snails

Steamed mussels

GRILLED CUTTLEFISH
Sepia a la plancha

This is a very traditional appetizer which tends to be cooked very well on the Mediterranean Coast. The muscles of the cuttlefish are very dense and can be tough and chewy when overcooked. I'll show you a few tricks to avoid ending up with a rubbery cuttlefish. It's usually served with aioli on toast.

SERVES 4
4 medium cuttlefish
3 peeled garlic cloves
2 Tbsp. chopped parsley
Spanish extra virgin olive oil
a pinch of salt for every cuttlefish
4 toast slices with aioli (see recipe on page 79)

1. To clean the cuttlefish, pull the tentacles gently away from the hood which should bring out the innards as well. Remove and discard the beak. Remove the soft bone from the hood. Wash under running water. Pull the skin away and discard it.
2. Peel the garlic cloves and crush in a mortar. Add the parsley and a pinch of salt. Continue crushing until you get a homogeneous paste.
3. Pour 50 ml. (3 Tbsp.) of olive oil slowly while stirring the paste with the pestle.
4. Here are 3 tips for a tender cuttlefish:
   - Buy good quality cuttlefish, as it is considerably more tender than cheap cuttlefish.
   - Freeze and then defrost before cooking.
   - Scrape off as much skin as you can. It will come off in thin sheets.
5. Fry it quickly, about 1-2 minutes on each side in hot oil (2 Tbsp.) over a medium-high heat.
6. Fry until the flesh is white or light golden and no longer translucent.
7. Spoon the garlic sauce over the cuttlefish and serve immediately with aioli on toast.
8. In Spanish bars and restaurants, it is very often served already cut into small chunks. Delicious!

BATTERED SQUID
Calamares rebozados / Rabas

This recipe is very typical on the coastal regions of Spain. In Northern Spain, they use the term "rabas" and in the rest of the country "Calamares Rebozados". They come in different shapes: sometimes in rings and sometimes in long strips. You'll find them in any bar because there's nothing more Spanish than eating "calamares" as an appetizer or tapa before lunch on a weekend.

SERVES 4
300 gr. (11 oz.) clean squid or squid rings
100 gr. (3.5 oz.) flour
140 ml. (5 fl. oz.) water
Spanish extra virgin olive oil
1/2 lemon or lemon wedges (optional)
salt to taste

1. Clean the squid like you would clean a cuttlefish (see previous recipe). Cut off the tentacles.
2. Cut the body with scissors into rings of about 1 cm. (1/3 inch). You can also buy the squid already cleaned and in rings. Frozen squid rings are also a great alternative. Just unthaw them before starting the recipe.
3. If you want the squid in strips, cut the rings in half.
4. Sift the flour into a bowl and add the water slowly while stirring with a fork or a whisk. You should get a thick paste. The amount of water may vary depending on the type of flour. If you see the mixture is too thick or too runny, add a bit of water or flour accordingly. It should have the texture of a tempura/ crepes batter.
5. Press the squid in your hands so all the water in them comes out. Dry with kitchen roll or cloth. Season with salt to taste.
6. Dip a handful of squid rings/strips in the batter.
7. Heat up a good amount of olive oil in a small frying pan or pot. The best is to deep fry them in small batches. When it's hot, place the squid into the pan with a fork one by one. Fry them over a medium-high heat until golden brown on all sides.
8. Using a slotted spoon, lift out the squid rings, holding them briefly over the pan to allow the excess oil to drain. Transfer to a paper towel lined plate to drain further. Serve with a lemon wedge.

GALICIAN STYLE OCTOPUS Pulpo a la Gallega

This is one of the most popular and spectacular recipes in Spain's gastronomy. So unique and utterly delicious, that everyone that tries this dish, falls in love with it immediately. Here I´m going to give you the true original Galician style method of cooking octopus. First of all, use a good quality octopus, the best one naturally coming from Galicia in Northern Spain. You will recognize its distinctive feature of two rows of suction cups on the undersides of the tentacles, while other species either have one or three rows.

SERVES 4
1 octopus
500 gr. (1 lb.) potatoes
1 tsp. sweet paprika
Spanish extra virgin olive oil
salt to taste

1. First freeze it. This will ensure that the octopus is tender when cooked, unless you want to try banging it against some rocks like octopus fishermen do!
2. Bring a large tall pot with unsalted water to boil. Don't add salt to the water as if you boil the octopus in salty water it won't be tender.
3. Now you must "scare" the octopus in the following way: when the water is boiling rapidly, holding the octopus by the head, dip the entire length of the tentacles into the water for 5 seconds and then remove it. See how the tentacles curl up. Repeat this four times and then immerse the whole octopus leaving it to boil at a medium heat uncovered. This trick will keep the skin tight to the octopus flesh so it doesn't flake or break.
4. Leave the octopus in the boiling water. If you like, you can also add 2 peeled medium potatoes. For how long do you have to boil the octopus and potatoes? It depends on the weight of the octopus. The rule is 18 minutes per kilo (2.2 lb.).
5. After you´ve boiled it for the appropriate time, remove the pot from the heat and leave the octopus in the water for 10 more minutes. Take out the octopus. If the potatoes are not tender by then, boil them for longer.
6. Slice the potatoes and place them on a platter. However, note that the traditional recipe uses a wooden round board as a platter. Cut the octopus tentacles in 3mm slices with scissors and lay them over the potatoes. Sprinkle sweet paprika generously all over and pour over a good drizzle of extra virgin olive oil.
7. If you follow these steps, you will have a tasty, tender and unforgettable Galician Octopus experience.

TIP: Combine with a glass of Albariño white wine, the typical and delicious white wine from Galicia.

RAZOR CLAMS IN GARLIC SAUCE Navajas con ajolio

SERVES 4
1 kg. (2.2 lb.) razor clams
3 peeled garlic cloves
2 sprigs of parsley, ground
Spanish extra virgin olive oil
a pinch of sea salt

1. Wash the razor clams under running water and then place them in a large bowl with water for 2 hours to get rid of the sand. Change the water at least 3 times, getting rid of the sand each time. I usually place a strainer in the bowl so I can take out the clams while leaving the sand in the bowl.
2. Peel the garlic cloves and crush in a mortar. Add the parsley and a pinch of salt. Continue crushing until you get a homogeneous paste.
3. Pour 50 ml. (3 Tbsp.) of olive oil slowly while stirring the paste with the pestle.
4. In a medium pot, heat the water with 1 Tbsp. of salt over a high heat. Bring to boil and then add the razor clams. You can also use a steamer instead of a pot.
5. Cook covered until razor clams have opened wide (about 3-5 minutes). Discard any that are closed.
6. Spoon the garlic sauce over the razor clam meat.

CLAMS IN GREEN SAUCE Almejas en salsa verde

This Spanish dish is usually served as a starter on special occasions. The green sauce is very common in the Basque Country and is used in many important recipes in the Spanish gastronomy but this recipe is also very popular along the whole Mediterranean Coast Regions.

SERVES 4
1 kg. (2.2 lb.) clams
3 medium garlic cloves
a handful of fresh parsley
50 ml. (3 Tbsp.) Spanish extra virgin olive oil
1 Tbsp. flour
125 ml. (1/2 cup) white wine
a pinch of salt

1. Soak the clams in a large bowl of water for 1 hour to get rid of the sand. Change the water at least 3 times, getting rid of the sand each time. I like placing a strainer in the bowl so it's easier to take out the clams and leave the sand in the bowl.
2. Peel the garlic cloves and crush in a mortar. Add the parsley and a pinch of salt. Continue crushing until you get a homogeneous paste.
3. Pour 50 ml. (3 Tbsp.) of olive oil slowly while stirring the paste with the pestle.
4. Spoon the garlic sauce from the mortar into a large pan and cook over a medium heat.
5. Pour a cup of water (225 ml.) into the mortar. Stir it with a fork.
6. When the garlic oil is warm in the pan, add the flour and fry over a medium heat until golden (about 1 minute). Pour a glass of white wine and the water from the mortar into the pan. Stir well.
7. Bring to a gentle boil. Rinse the clams under running water and then add them to the pan. Stir and combine the clams with the sauce. Cover with a lid and cook over medium heat.
8. Cook until the clams have opened wide (about 5 minutes). Discard any clams that don't open.
9. I recommend you get yourself a nice baguette, because this green sauce is really outstanding and moreish. You won't be able to stop dipping.

BOILED SEA SNAILS Caracoles de mar

This dish might sound rather exotic but it is very popular along the Spanish Coast. A lot of people who don't like earth snails, love sea snails. Give it a try if visiting Spain.

SERVES 4
1 kg. (2.2 lb.) sea snails
2/3 litres (3 cups) water
1 Tbsp. sea salt

1. Rinse the sea snails under cold water.
2. In a medium pot, heat the water with 1 Tbsp. of salt over a high heat. Bring to a boil and add in the snails. Lower the heat to medium-low. Cover the pot. Cook the sea snails for about 15 minutes. Ideally you could boil them (as with all seafood) in sea water.
3. Drain them and serve.
4. Instructions to eat sea snails:
   Using a snail fork or toothpick, pull the snail out of the shell gently. Most of the time, the snail body will separate from the intestinal tract which will remain in the shell. The intestinal tract is mushy but the edible body is rubbery. Sometimes you'll have to separate both parts using your finger.
   Pull off the hard foot (cover) on top of the sea snail. Eat the body meat and enjoy.

SHRIMP GARLIC STYLE
Gambas al ajillo

This recipe comes originally from the Basque Country and is sometimes served with "gulas", baby-eel-like strips of grey "surimi". It is usually served in individual clay dishes as an appetizer or tapa but also as a first course.

SERVES 4
600 gr. (1.3 lb.) peeled raw shrimps
1 cayenne pepper
4 garlic cloves, peeled and sliced
Spanish extra virgin olive oil
handful of chopped parsley (optional)
salt to taste

1. Wash the shrimps and dry them well.
2. Heat 4 Tbsp. of olive oil in a frying pan over a medium heat. Fry the cayenne pepper and garlic cloves until light golden. Be careful because they can burn really quickly.
3. Add in the shrimps and fry turning them over half way through. Season with salt. You should fry the shrimps for 3 minutes in total.
4. If you can find "gulas" and you would like to use them, add them in the frying pan 1 minute before you finish cooking the shrimps.
5. You can also sprinkle chopped parsley on top.

GRILLED PRAWNS
Langostinos a la plancha

This is one of the most common starters on coastal regions. The quality of the fresh prawns fished in Spain is very high and important for this recipe. You could always try making it with good quality frozen ones. A tip to check if a cooked prawn is fresh: when you peel it, the shell should come off easily; if it's difficult to peel, it's not fresh.

SERVES 4
16 fresh unpeeled raw shrimps
salt to taste
2 Tbsp. Spanish extra virgin olive oil

1. Wash the shrimps and dry them well.
2. Heat 2 Tbsp. of olive oil in a frying pan over a medium-high heat. Turn the shrimps over in the pan when the oil is hot and fry them in several batches (shrimps should fit in one layer). The moment you turn them, lower the heat to medium. Season with salt and fry for about 2 minutes until they start to turn pink around the edges. Turn over and season with salt again. Fry 2 more minutes.
3. Serve immediately.
4. Eat them with your hands like so: Hold the shrimp in one hand, between the thumb and forefinger. With your free hand grasp the sides of the head with the thumb and forefinger and twist so it comes off. Pull the legs and shell off the shrimp. They should easily slip off in one piece.

STEAMED MUSSELS
Mejillones al vapor

This is the most common way of cooking mussels in Spain because it's quick, easy and delicious. This recipe brings out the exquisite and intense flavor of the mussels. It can be eaten as a second course or as a tapa. You can also use them as the basis for more elaborate mussels recipes.

SERVES 4
1 kg. (2.2 lb.) mussels
2 bay leaves
250 ml. (1 cup) of water
1 Tbsp. sea salt
1 lemon wedge
50 ml. (3 Tbsp.) white wine (optional)

1. Rinse the mussels well under cold water. Pull off or cut off with scissors any beards. Discard any mussels that are broken or gaping open.
2. In a medium pot, heat the water with 1 Tbsp. of salt over a high heat. Bring to boil and then add the mussels. You can also use a steamer instead of a pot.
3. Add the bay leaves and white wine (if using) and cover the pot. Cook until the mussels have opened wide (about 3-5 minutes).
4. Drain the mussels. Discard any closed mussels.
5. Serve immediately with a lemon wedge.

TAPAS

IBERIAN HAM CROQUETTES (62)

BRAVE POTATOES (63)

STUFFED SPANISH OMELETTE (63)

CURED HAM TOAST (63)

COURGETTE & MUSHROOM TOAST (64)

SMALL TUNA EMPANADAS (64)

MUSHROOM PUFF PASTRY (64)

FRIED PRAWNS IN BATTER (65)

POTATO PUREE BOMBS (65)

Mushroom puff pastry

Small tuna empanadas

Cured ham toast

Stuffed Spanish omelette

Courgette & mushroom toast

Fried prawns in batter

Brave potatoes

Iberian ham croquettes

Potato puree bombs

IBERIAN HAM CROQUETTES

Croquetas de Jamón Ibérico

This is a delicious croquette recipe, made with ham and onions. You can't visit a Spanish bar without seeing this tapa under the glass counter. And they can be made with so many different ingredients: cod, funghi, shrimps, boiled eggs, etc. There are no limits.

MAKES ABOUT 20 CROQUETTES
1 onion
200 gr. Spanish cured ham
2 beaten eggs
100 gr. (3.5 oz.) wheat flour
100 gr. (3.5 oz.) breadcrumbs
Spanish extra virgin olive oil
For the bechamel:
110 gr. (4 oz.) wheat flour
110 gr. (4 oz.) margarine
1 liter of cold milk
salt to taste

1. Fry 1 finely chopped onion in a medium frying pan with 1 Tbsp. olive oil over a medium heat until tender. Take out the onion with as little as oil as possible. Set aside.
2. Finely slice the cured ham with a knife.
3. To make the bechamel, follow recipe of thick bechamel on page 80.
4. Once you've prepared the béchamel in a pot or saucepan, mix in the onion and ham. Cook covered for about 5 minutes.
5. Spoon the bechamel sauce onto a plate. Spread the mixture evenly. Let it cool for 30 minutes. Then you can either brush the surface with margarine or cover it with cling film touching the surface. That will prevent the formation of a skin. Refrigerate for at least 3 hours.
6. Prepare 3 plates: one with flour, another with beaten egg and the last one with breadcrumbs.
7. Cut a small portion of the cold bechamel with a knife or spoon and place it on the plate with the flour. Cover your hands with flour so the croquettes don't stick. Shape the croquettes into any shape and size you like (fingers, balls, oval shape...). Roll the croquette in the flour, shaking off any excess.
8. Press the croquette on the plate with the beaten egg and dip it. With a fork, roll it so it gets completely coated by the egg.
9. Lift it from the egg and roll it in the bread crumbs coating it evenly.
10. Heat up a good amount of olive oil in a frying pan over a high-medium heat. The amount of oil depends on the size of the pan. The oil must cover the bottom half of the croquettes and be quite hot at first. When it's hot (but before getting smoky hot) place them carefully in the oil. Lower the heat to a medium heat. Fry them in small batches. Turn them gently, for about 2 minutes, or until they are golden on all sides.
11. Using a slotted spoon, lift out the croquettes, holding them briefly over the pan to allow excess oil to drain, and transfer to a paper towel lined plate to drain further. Serve warm

TIP: Try using Japanese "Panko" breadcrumbs instead of regular breadcrumbs.

BRAVE POTATOES Patatas Bravas

This recipe has many versions with different sauces. The one I am going to show you here is very typical in the city of Zaragoza in Aragón and to my taste, is the best one.

SERVES 6
4 medium potatoes
Spanish extra virgin olive oil
a drizzle of tabasco (optional)
salt to taste
aioli (see recipe on page 79)

1. Pre-heat oven to 200°C (392°F).
2. Pre-heat oven. Peel and wash the potatoes. Cut into irregular medium chunks.
3. Place them on a baking tray and season with salt.
4. Pour olive oil all over the potato chunks. Give them a toss with your hands.
5. Roast in the oven in middle rack until golden and tender (about 20-30 minutes). Take out of the oven and place on plate or serving tray.
6. Make the aioli following recipe on page 79.
7. Add the tabasco sauce to the aioli and combine. Spoon the aioli over the potatoes.

STUFFED SPANISH OMELETTE Tortilla de patata rellena

This is taking the Spanish Omelette to the next level by filling it with tasty ingredients. There are countless variations. I discovered this version in the Basque Country and I must confess it's one of my favorites.

SERVES 4
One Spanish Potato Omelette (see page 22)
6 surimi sticks
2-4 Tbsp. mayonnaise (see page 79)

1. Make one Spanish Omelette following recipe on page 22.
2. Slide the omelette onto a large plate. Let it cool for 10 minutes. Cut into 6 portions. Slice each portion lengthwise.
3. Finely chop the surimi and combine with the mayonnaise.
4. Spread the mixture evenly on the bottom half of every omelette portion. Place the top halves on top, slightly pressing down.

CURED HAM TOAST Montadito de jamón

Spaniards have this as an everyday tapa but also as part of a very typical ordinary Spanish breakfast.

SERVES 1
1 ripe tomato
1 toast of bread
cured ham to taste
a drizzle of Spanish extra virgin olive oil

1. Wash a ripe tomato and cut it in half.
2. Cut a slice of crusty bread and toast it.
3. Rub one half tomato on the toast and drizzle with olive oil.
4. Place cured ham slices on top and enjoy!

COURGETTE & MUSHROOM TOAST
Tosta de calabacín y champiñón

MAKES 4 TOASTS
½ medium courgette
4 toasts of bread
4 large mushrooms
Spanish extra virgin olive oil
salt to taste
a pinch of ground black pepper
ground parsley to taste

1. Wash and slice the courgette. Fry in a pan with oil until tender. Remove and set aside.
2. Wash and press the mushrooms in your hand so the water in them comes out. Cut off their tails. Place in an oven tray and drizzle with oil and season with salt and pepper. Bake in preheated oven at 180°C (355°F) for 15-20 minutes.
3. To assemble, place each toast on a tray. Top them with the fried courgettes and then place the baked mushrooms on top.
4. Insert a long toothpick through the food to keep all ingredients together. Sprinkle parsley on top.

SMALL TUNA EMPANADAS
Empanadillas de atún

These typical Spanish Galician Empanadillas are forbidden food. And a must in any Spanish bar. They are usually made of tuna but you can also find them filled with other types of fish, ham and cheese or even other imaginative ingredients.

MAKES ABOUT 20 LITTLE EMPANADS
2 packs of puff pastry chilled approx. 300 gr. (10.5 oz.) each
150 gr. (5 oz.) canned tuna in olive oil, drained
1 small onion, finely diced
10 green olives (pitted and finely chopped)
200 ml. (7 fl. oz.) fried tomato puree
30 ml. (2 Tbsp.) milk
25 gr. (¼ cup) grated cheese
Spanish extra virgin olive oil
pinch of salt

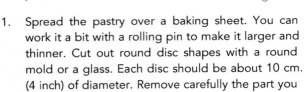

1. Spread the pastry over a baking sheet. You can work it a bit with a rolling pin to make it larger and thinner. Cut out round disc shapes with a round mold or a glass. Each disc should be about 10 cm. (4 inch) of diameter. Remove carefully the part you don't need.
2. Heat 2 lugs of olive oil in a frying pan (you could also use the olive oil from the tuna can). Fry the onion over a medium-low heat until tender.
3. Mix in the olives and the tuna. Combine well. Cook for a couple of minutes and pour in the fried tomato

puree and milk. Stir and cook for 3 minutes over a medium heat. Season with salt and combine.
4. Sprinkle the cheese over the mixture and cook until it melts, stirring constantly. Transfer the filling to a plate and let it cool for 10 minutes.
5. Place 1-2 Tbsp. of the filling on one half of each disc. Don't overfill it.
6. To seal the empanadas, fold the discs over and press down the edges of the dough with a fork. You can also brush the inside edges with beaten egg to help seal the empanadillas. Brush them with beaten egg if you want your empanadillas to have a nice golden finish.
7. Fry the empanadillas in a frying pan with enough oil to cover their bottom half. Fry over a medium heat until golden, turning once, about 1 minute. Take out and drain on a plate lined with a paper towel. Let them cool and enjoy!

MUSHROOM PUFF PASTRY
Hojaldradito de champiñón

This type of pastry called "vol-au-vent" is very common on Spanish bar counters. You can buy the pastry already made.

MAKES 6
6 vol-au-vents
75 gr. (2.6 oz.) mushrooms
1/2 shallot
1 ½ Tbsp. flour
200 ml. (7 fl. oz.) cold milk
3 Tbsp. Spanish extra virgin olive oil
a handful of parsley
ground black pepper to taste
salt to taste
6 pinches of grated cheese

1. Pre-heat oven to 180°C (355°F).
2. Wash the mushrooms and then press them in your hands to get rid of the water in them. Peel, wash and finely mince the shallot.
3. Heat up the olive oil in a pan, add the shallot and fry over a medium heat until tender. Add the mushrooms and fry all together for 3-5 minutes until all the moisture from the mushrooms dries up. Mix in the flour and fry for 2 minutes.
4. Pour in the milk and stir. Season with salt and pepper. Cook over a medium-low heat until the sauce thickens. Fill the vol-au-vents with the mushroom mixture. Sprinkle grated cheese and ground parsley on top of each pastry.
5. Cook in the oven in middle rack for 10 minutes at 180°C (355°F).

FRIED PRAWNS IN BATTER Gambas en gabardina

Literally it translates as "Prawns in a raincoat" which refers to the batter which coats the prawns before they are deep fried. When you visit a Spanish bar and spend some time there having a drink or a tapa, you will hear the waiter yell to the kitchen: "Una de gambas". That means somebody ordered "one batch of Prawns". You might hear that several times! Try out this recipe and you will know why.

MAKES 16 PRAWNS
16 raw unpeeled prawns
1 egg
8 gr. (2 tsp.) baking powder

80 gr. (3/4 cup) flour sifted
60 ml. (4 Tbsp.) beer
Spanish extra virgin olive oil
salt to taste

1. Wash the prawns and peel them, leaving the tail on. Dry them well with some kitchen roll. You can reserve/freeze the shells you peeled, to make seafood stock (see page 78).
2. Season the prawns with salt.
3. In a bowl, beat an egg with a fork or a hand whisk.Pour in the beer and mix again
4. Add the flour, baking powder and a pinch of salt a little at a time while whisking by hand so you don't get any lumps.
5. This batter is called "Orly" and must have crepe batter consistency. Not too thick and not too runny. If necessary, add more beer little by little to get that consistency.
6. Heat up a good amount of olive oil in a frying pan over a high-medium heat. The amount of oil depends on the size of the pan. The oil must cover the bottom half of the prawns and be quite hot at first. When it's hot (but before getting smoky hot) hold each prawn by its tail, quickly dip it into the batter mix and place them carefully in the oil. Lower the heat to a medium heat. Fry them in small batches. Turn them gently, for about 1minute each side, or until they are golden on both sides.
7. Using a slotted spoon, lift out the prawns, holding them briefly over the pan to allow excess oil to drain, and transfer to a paper towel lined plate to drain further. Serve warm.

POTATO PUREE BOMBS Bombas de Patata

You can find stuffed potato puree "Bombs" everywhere in Spain. They are available with all sorts of ingredients and the most common ones usually contain minced meat or flaked canned tuna.

SERVES 4
1 kg. (2.2 lb.) medium potatoes
250 gr. (9 oz.) minced meat (half beef, half pork)
1 small onion, finely minced
6 Tbsp. tomato puree
a drizzle of Worcester Sauce

salt to taste
ground black pepper to taste
Spanish extra virgin olive oil
For the Batter:
2 beaten eggs
100 gr. (3.5 oz.) breadcrumbs

1. Wash the potatoes. Bring a pot of salted water to a boil and carefully add in the potatoes. Make sure they are covered completely by the water. Cook until tender (about 25-35 minutes depending on hardness, type and size of the potatoes). Drain and let cool for 20 minutes.
2. Peel the potatoes. Using an electric beater or potato masher, blend the potatoes with 1 Tbsp. of olive oil in a bowl until smooth. Refrigerate for 20 minutes.
3. Meanwhile, heat 2 Tbsp. of olive oil in a large saucepan over a medium-high heat and fry the minced meat with the minced onion until cooked. Season with salt and black pepper.
4. Add in the tomato puree and the Worcester Sauce and combine well. Cook for 5 minutes, stirring occasionally. Transfer to a plate and let it cool for 10 minutes.
5. Take one spoonful of puree and form a half ball with your hands. Form a hole in the middle with your finger and layer in about 1 Tbsp. of the meat filling. Top it with more potato puree to completely form a ball. Repeat for every ball.
6. Roll the balls on a plate with 2 beaten eggs so they are completely coated by the eggs. Coat in breadcrumbs.
7. Heat up a good amount of olive oil in a frying pan over a high-medium heat. The amount of oil depends on the size of the pan. The oil must cover the bottom half of the "Bombs" and be quite hot at first. When it's hot (but before getting smoky hot) place them carefully in the oil. Lower the heat to a medium heat. Fry them in small batches. Turn them gently, for about 1 minute, or until they are golden on all sides. Using a slotted spoon, lift out the "Bombs", holding them briefly over the pan to allow excess oil to drain, and transfer to a paper towel lined plate to drain further. Serve warm. You can top them with mayonnaise and/or tomato puree.

DESSERTS

Three wise men cake

Spanish sweet bread

Churros

Homemade yoghurt sponge cake

Sweet fritters

Apple tarts

Santiago cake

Small sweet empanadas

Puff pastry honey ribbons

Egg flan

Mallorcan snail pastries

Catalan creme brulée

THREE WISE MEN CAKE Roscón de Reyes

This is a traditional cake eaten for breakfast or dessert on the 6th of January to celebrate the day when the three Wise Men came to leave presents for the baby Jesus. This is also the day when Spanish children receive their Christmas presents. You can make it with or without filling, although the one with whipped cream is the most popular. A small surprise present is hidden in the dough or the filling. Whoever finds it, has to buy the cake (or bake it) next year. The cake is mostly frequently prepared in a large ring shape but can also be prepared in 8 individual cakes. The only difference is that you have to cut the dough into balls after it has risen for the first time and then you follow the same instructions as for the large ring.

SERVES 8-10
For the dough:
500 gr. (2 cups) all purpose flour
100 gr. (1/2 cup) granulated sugar
100 gr. (1/2 cup) butter melted
25 gr. (0.9 oz.) baker's yeast
2 eggs
220 ml. (1 cup) milk
1 tsp. grated orange zest
1 tsp. orange blossom water (only if you can find it)
pinch of salt
For decoration:
1 beaten egg
a handful chopped toasted almonds
candied mixed fruits
granulated sugar
powdered sugar
For the filling (optional):
250 ml (1 cup) whipping cream
1-2 Tbsp. granulated sugar

1. Mix all ingredients together in a large bowl and stir well with a fork. You can also use your hands. Cover the dough with cling film and leave to rise in a warm place (near a radiator) until it almost doubles in size, about 1h30min - 2h30min.
2. Place the dough on a floured surface and knead for 2 to 3 minutes. Shape the dough into a ring. You can also cut it into 6 little dough balls. This is the moment when you hide the surprise (tiny figurine) in the dough (if you prefer not to make the cake with whipped cream filling).
3. Line an oven dish with baking paper and place the ring on it. Brush the surface gently with the beaten egg. Arrange the candied mixed fruit and almonds on top, pushing them slightly into the dough. Sprinkle wet sugar all over the ring.
4. Let the dough rise again in a warm place until it almost doubles in size (about 2 hours). Place a ring mold in the middle to keep the ring shape.
5. Pre-heat the oven to 340°F (170°C) for 10 minutes. Take out the ring mold form the centre of the dough ring. Place the ring in the middle rack and bake for 13-15 minutes. If you see after 5 minutes that the top gets too brown before the bottom part is cooked, cover the ring with tin foil. This way you'll be able to bake it completely without burning the top.
6. Take it out and let it cool for 10 minutes. In case you want to fill it with whipped cream, let the ring cool 10 more minutes.
7. You need to use stable whipped cream and you can achieve that either by:

    a. Using cream which is at least 35% percent fat.
    b. Adding dry milk powder before whipping. Stir in 2 tsp (10 ml.) milk powder for each cup (240 ml./1 cup) cream.
    c. Chilling all ingredients and tools at least 30 minutes before whipping. The colder the cream, the less likely it is to separate. Make sure the tools are dry.

8. Whip the cream in a large cold bowl with an electric mixer until soft peaks form. Sift 1 to 2 Tbsp. of granulated sugar over cream; beat until soft peaks return. Do not overbeat.
9. Finally cut the ring lengthwise with a knife. Lift the top part and layer with whipped cream. This is the moment to hide the surprise in the cream filling.
10. Sprinkle powdered sugar on top of the "roscón". Enjoy!

SANTIAGO CAKE Tarta de Santiago

The Santiago Cake happens to be a gluten free cake as it is made with ground almonds instead of flour. Isn't that great? But this is no ordinary almond cake. It's so moist, scrumptious and easy to make that you won't want to stop making it again and again. In my house, it doesn't last more than a day! This cake is very popular and well known all over Spain but its origins are in the Galician city of Santiago de Compostela where the apostle Santiago's body lies. That is why it is usually marked with the shape of the cross of the Order of Santiago.

SERVE 6
250 gr. (8.8 oz.) almonds
5 large eggs
½ tsp. lemon zest
1/4 tsp. ground cinnamon
1 Tbsp. anisette
unsalted butter or oil to grease
250 gr. (8.8 oz.) powdered sugar + more to dust

1. Pre-heat oven to 120°C. I like grinding the almonds in two batches. I grind the first batch very very finely until I get a sort of "almond flour". I then grind the second batch less finely so that I can feel the almonds crunch between my teeth when eating the cake. Line an oven tray with baking paper and spread the ground almonds. Roast in the middle rack of the oven for 10 minutes.

2. In a large bowl, beat the sugar and eggs with a hand whisk into a pale cream. Beat in the zest, cinnamon and anisette. Let the roast almonds cool and then add them into the bowl, mixing well with a spatula.

3. Grease with butter a 9 inch (23 cm. approx.) spring form pan. Pour the cake mix into the pan and bake in middle rack in a pre-heated oven (180°C) for 35 minutes or until a needle comes out clean. Let it cool before un-molding.

4. Cut a cross of the Order of Santiago out of paper or thin cardboard. Place it on the cake and dust it with powdered sugar. Carefully remove the paper.

HOMEMADE YOGHURT SPONGE CAKE Bizcocho de yogur casero

This is a very popular recipe in Spanish homes. All measures are calculated with a 125 ml. (1/2 cup) empty yoghurt container. Really easy!

SERVES 8-10
(125 ml./1/2 cup) 1 natural flavor yoghurt
3 eggs
3 measures of sifted flour
2 measures of sugar
1 measure of olive oil
15 gr. (1 Tbsp.). baking powder
a pinch of salt
powdered sugar for decoration

1. Pre-heat the oven to 170°C (325°F).
2. Put the sugar, eggs, yoghurt and oil in a free standing electric mixer with a paddle attachment (or use a whisk) and beat until ingredients are well incorporated. Add the sifted flour, baking powder and salt a little at a time while beating. Beat until well mixed.
3. Pour the mixture into a 23 cm. (9 inch) baking tray, greased with a bit of oil.
4. Bake in the pre-heated oven for 20-25 min. or until golden brown and an inserted needle comes out clean. Let it cool before un-molding. Sprinkle powdered sugar on top.

TIP: Try different yoghurt flavors like lemon. You could also add in ¼ tsp. vanilla extract

---

SPANISH SWEET BREAD Torrijas

This is a sweet delicacy that Spaniards eat especially as a dessert or afternoon snack during Easter. It dates back to the 15th century and is believed to have been created in the convents to use up stale bread. There are many variations but here I'm going to show you the original recipe.

SERVES 6
12 slices of stale baguette or crusty bread
500 ml. (2 cups) of milk
1 cinnamon stick
1 lemon peel
4 Tbsp. sugar
2 beaten eggs
wheat flour
1 Tbsp. ground cinnamon
Spanish extra virgin olive oil

1. Cut the bread into slices approximately 3/4 of an inch (2 cm.) thick.
2. Heat the milk in a sauce pan over a medium-high heat. Add 2 Tbsp. of sugar, the lemon peel and cinnamon stick. Stir to dilute the sugar. Bring to boil and then remove from heat.
3. Pass the milk through a sieve. Place a bowl underneath it. Let it cool for 5-10 minutes.
4. Place the bread slices on a plate and with a spoon or a ladle, pour the milk from the bowl over each slice. Turn the bread over and pour milk over again to make sure the slices are completely soaked, even the crust. The inside of the bread should be mushy.
5. Start heating up a good amount of extra virgin olive oil in a small frying pan over a high-medium heat. Prepare a plate with flour and another one with 2 beaten eggs. Coat each bread slice in the flour shaking off any excess.
6. Dip both sides of the slices in the beaten eggs.
7. When the olive oil is hot, lower the heat to medium and start frying the torrijas. The oil should cover the bottom half of the bread. When the bottom of the bread begins to slightly brown (about 1 minute) turn them over.
8. Fry until golden on both sides. Take them out of the frying pan using a slotted spoon.
9. Transfer to a paper towel lined plate to drain the excess oil. Let them cool for 2 minutes.
10. Mix 2 Tbsp. of sugar with 1 Tbsp. of ground cinnamon in a small bowl or plate. Stir well with a fork. Coat the torrijas all over by rolling them in the sugar-cinnamon mixture. Serve and enjoy.

CHURROS

Is there any other Spanish treat more famous than churros? I don't think so. They come in different shapes and sizes: straight, curved sticks and ribbon shaped. You can find them in any corner of the country but they are considered to have originated in Madrid. Spaniards have them frequently for breakfast or in the afternoon accompanied with hot chocolate (sometimes with whipped cream on top of the hot chocolate).

SERVES 4
250 gr. (2 cups.) universal flour
500 ml. (2 cups) water
granulated sugar to taste
Spanish extra virgin olive oil
a pinch of salt

1. Bring the water to a boil with a pinch of salt in a pot.
2. Spoon in the flour at once when it starts boiling.
3. Stir with a wooden spoon until the mixture gets thick enough to allow the wooden spoon to stand on its own in the middle of the mixture. Remove from the heat and let it cool for 10 minutes.
4. Spoon mixture into a cookie maker or pastry bag fitted with a large open-star tip.
5. Heat up a good amount of olive oil in a small frying pan or a small pot over a high-medium heat. The amount of oil depends on the size of the pan or pot. I like to use a pot as a fryer adding as much oil as it needs to cover the churros. When it's hot (but before getting smoky hot). holding the pastry bag a few inches above the oil, squeeze out the mixture, snipping off 10 cm. (4 inch) lengths with scissors or wet fingertips. Fry, turning once, until deep golden brown all over, about 4 minutes. Using a slotted spoon, transfer churros to a paper towel-lined baking sheet to drain.
6. Lower the heat to a medium heat. Fry them in small batches. After 2 minutes, sprinkle sugar all over the churros.

PUFF PASTRY HONEY RIBBONS
Lazos de hojaldre con miel

These ribbons are as beautiful as they are scrumptious. They can be easily found all over Spain in bakeries, supermarkets and delicatessen shops. You can imagine how wonderful the homebaked ones are.

SERVES 4
2 rectangular puff pastry sheets of 250 gr. (8.8 oz.) each
2-3 Tbsp. condensed milk
50 gr. (1.7 oz) honey
45 ml. (3 Tbsp.) water
flour
powdered sugar

1. Heat the honey and water over a medium-low heat in a pot. Bring to a gentle boil and remove from heat. Let it cool.
2. Pre-heat the oven to 200°C (390°F).
3. Take the puff pastries out of the fridge. Roll them out on a lightly floured surface with a roller pin.
4. Brush one puff pastry with condensed milk.
5. Spoon the honey-water mix over the same puff pastry which you covered with condensed milk. Spoon just enough so there's honey everywhere. Place the other puff pastry sheet on top of the one you have covered with milk and honey.
6. Cut the whole pastry into long vertical stripes about 2.5 cm (1 inch) wide from the top to the bottom of the pastry.
7. Now cut the pastry perpendicularly in half.
8. Twist each stripe in your hands into a ribbon shape like the ones you see in the picture.
9. Place each ribbon on an oven tray lined with baking paper. Brush the surface of the ribbons with the remaining honey-water mix.
10. Bake in pre-heated oven at 200°C (390°) in middle rack for 12-15 minutes until golden on the outside.
11. Take them out and let cool. Sift a generous amount of powdered sugar all over the ribbons. ¡Que aproveche!

APPLE TARTS Pastelitos de manzana

MAKES 5-6 TARTS
2 apples
1 sheet of puff pastry (pack chilled)
250 ml. (1 cup) milk
2 egg yolks
60 gr. (4 Tbsp..) sugar
16 gr. (0.8 oz.) wheat flour
12 gr. (0.4 oz.) corn flour
½ tsp. lemon zest
1/2 vanilla pod
6 sour cherries
2 Tbsp. apricot jam

1. First of all, prepare the custard cream: whisk the wheat flour, corn flour and sugar in a bowl. Add the egg yolks and 50 ml. (2 Tbsp.) of milk and mix into a smooth paste. I recommend sifting both flours beforehand to avoid any lumps.

2. In a saucepan, heat the remaining milk with the vanilla pod and lemon zest over a medium heat until scalding hot and about to boil. But be careful. It shouldn't reach boiling point. Take out the vanilla pod and lemon zest with a sieve. Pour the paste from the bowl into the scalding sauce pan.

3. Set the saucepan over a low heat. Whisk constantly and also scrape the bottom of the pan at the same time with a wooden spatula to stop the paste from sticking to the bottom and getting burnt. Don't let it boil. Cook until it thickens. Pour into a bowl and let it cool for 10 minutes.

4. Pre-heat the oven 200°C (392°F). Spread the pastry over a baking sheet on a tray. Using a knife, cut out oval shapes from the pasty with a margin like in the picture below. Fold the borders with your fingers.

5. Prick the base of the little tarts to avoid the center rising up.

6. Spread the custard cream on every tart. Peel and cut the apples into thin slices. Place them and the sour cherry on top. Brush the tarts all over with a mix of 2 Tbsp. apricot jam and a bit of water. Put in the oven on the middle rack for around 15 minutes or until golden.

SMALL SWEET EMPANADAS Pastissets

These pastries of arab origin can only be found in the Valencian and southern Catalan regions. They can have different fillings but the one in this recipe is the classic one and my personal favourite. They are very unique as they have a sandy consistency and they flake in your mouth.

SERVES 8
500 gr. (4 cups) baker's flour, sifted
200 ml.(1 cup) olive oil
45 ml. (3 Tbsp.) sweet Muscatel wine
45 ml. (3 Tbsp.) anisette
300 gr. (10 oz.) pumpkin strands jam (see recipe on page 73)
granulated sugar

1. Pre-heat oven to 180°C (390°F).
2. In a bowl, whisk the olive oil, muscatel wine and anisette until well combined.
3. Add the sifted flour a little at a time while whisking vigorously until the dough separates easily from the bowl. Then place the dough onto a floured surface and keep kneading.
4. Cut into 50 gr. (1.7 oz.) pieces and form balls with your hands.
5. Place a baking sheet on the kitchen counter. Place one ball on it and then cover the ball with another baking sheet on top. With a rollin pin, flatten the ball so you get a disc shaped dough. Remove the top baking sheet. Place 1-2 tsp. of the pumpkin strands in syrup on one half of the disc. Don´t overfill it. Fold the disc and seal the edges by pressing down the dough with fingers shaping a rim. (Look at the picture on page 66). Repeat this process with every ball.
6. Line a baking tray with baking paper. Place every pastisset on it. Bake in different batches (about 9 pastissets per batch). Bake in middle rack at 180 °C (390°F) for 20 minutes or until golden brown.
7. Take out of the oven and spray with anisette. (I recommend you pour anisette in a spray bottle).
8. Place 2 Tbsp. of sugar in a small bowl or plate and coat the Pastissets all over by rolling them in the sugar.

TIP: If you can't find Muscatel wine, you can use sweet sherry as a substitute.

SWEEET FRITTERS Pestiños

Pestiños are traditional Spanish pastries which are most commonly eaten in the period just before Lent, often during Carnival and also for Christmas. A Pestiño is a dough which is deep fried in olive oil and glazed with honey or sugar. It is very popular and easy to find all over Spain but especially in Andalusia due to its Muslim origins.

SERVES 6
1 kg. (2.2 lb.) all purpose flour
150 ml. (1/2 cup) sherry wine
150 ml. (1/2 cup) orange juice
100 gr. (3.5 oz.) roasted aniseed
100 gr. (3.5 oz.) sesame seeds
40 ml. (3 Tbsp.) anisette
1 lemon zest
1 orange zest
1 tsp ground cinnamon
a pinch of nutmeg
1 clove
a pinch of salt
Spanish olive oil
honey or white sugar depending on your preference

1. Heat 300 ml. (1 ¼ cups) of olive oil with the aniseed, sesame seeds, lemon and orange zests and clove until slightly golden. Pour the olive oil into a large bowl while draining through a sieve. Now the olive oil has the flavors of the ingredients. Let the oil cool completely.
2. Add the orange juice, sherry wine, cinnamon, nutmeg and anisette to the olive oil while stirring. Slowly add the flour into the oil and combine well until you get an elastic dough. You have to take into consideration that the amount of flour is approximate. Add as much flour as the dough can handle.
3. Place the dough on a floured surface and knead until you get a soft dough (a few minutes)
4. Roll dough about 1/8 inch thick and cut into 5 cm x 5 cm (2 inch x 2 inch) squares. Take two opposite corners from each square and press these together in the center. A trick to help you stick the corners together is adding a bit of water.
5. Heat up a good amount of olive oil in a small frying pan or skillet. When it's hot (but not smoky hot) fry the pestiños. Using a slotted spoon, lift them out, holding them briefly over the pan to allow the excess oil to drain and transfer to a paper towel lined plate to drain further.
6. Warm up 1 cup of honey with 2 Tbsp. of water and dip the pestiños in the warm honey-water. You can also just coat them in white sugar like in the picture on page 67.

SPANISH PUMPKIN STRANDS JAM Cabello de ángel

1 medium "cidra","cayote" or "spaghetti" squash or pumpkin
granulated sugar
1 cinnamon stick
lemon peel (5 cm./2 inches long)

1. Cut the squash in half and spoon out the seeds.
2. Simmer covered with a lid in a pot with hot water until flesh is tender but the squash still holds it's shape (about 5-10 minutes). Drain and allow to cool.
3. Scrape the cooked flesh from the skin and weigh.
4. Place the squash flesh in a pan or pot and add 3/4 of it's weight in sugar. For instance, if you had 1000 gr. (2.2 lb.) of boiled squash flesh, you would add 750 gr. (1.65 lb.) of sugar.
5. Add the cinnamon stick and lemon peel. Cook over a medium-low heat for about 1 hour, stirring occasionally. At first, it will look runny. It will be done when most of the liquid is evaporated and the pumpkin fibers are visible and golden.
6. Remove from the heat and leave to settle for 15 minutes or so. Pour into sterilized, dry, hot jars filling them almost to the top. Put the jar in a bath of boiling water for 15 minutes to create a vacuum. Dry and store out of sunlight.

LOVERS' SIGHS Suspiros de Amante

These lovers' sighs are a very typical sweet treat from Teruel. Their name refers to a love story that is supposed to have taken place in that beautiful town in 1217. It is as tragic and as romantic as Romeo and Juliet's story, and it has gained fame and popularity internationally. In fact, many tourists go to Teruel to visit the tombs of the lovers.

For the mini shortcrust tarts:
220 gr. (1 cup) plain flour
2 Tbsp. icing sugar
1 tsp. salt
150 gr. (5.3 oz.) cold block of unsalted butter
ice cold water
For the filling:
100 gr. (3.5 oz.) butter
45 gr. (3 Tbsp.) sugar
125 gr. (4.5 oz.) cream cheese
2 beaten eggs
icing sugar to decorate

1. In a large bowl, whisk in the flour, icing sugar and salt. Set aside.
2. Place a piece of greaseproof paper on both top and the bottom of the block of butter and bash it with a rolling pin. Once you've flattened it, break it up into the flour.
3. Rub the flour and butter together by picking up the flour pieces and butter together and pushing them through your fingers and thumbs, breaking them up and creating little flakes. When it reaches a breadcrumb consistency, add 3 Tbps. of ice cold water and stir with a metal fork until you are able to squeeze a bit between your fingers and it sticks together.
4. Squeeze the dough in the bowl until it gets all into one ball. Place the dough on a floured surface and kneed for a few seconds with your hands. Leave it to rest for at least 2 hours wrapped in cling film.
5. Pre-heat the oven to 180°C (390°F). Brush each mold with oil.
6. Dust the surface and rolling pin with flour. Cut into 50 gr. (1.7 oz.) pieces and form balls with your hands.
7. Place a baking sheet on the kitchen counter. Place one ball on it and then cover the ball with another baking sheet on top. With a rolling pin, flatten the ball of dough so you get a 2.5 mm. (1 inch) thick disc shape. Remove the top baking sheet. Repeat for each ball.
8. Place each disc in the mold and push them in. Make sure to push into the corners of the molds with your knuckles. Trim the edges with a sharp knife. Prick the bottom with a fork. Lay a sheet of greaseproof paper over the dough crust and pour in baking beans. Bake for about 10 minutes. Remove the greaseproof paper and baking beans and bake for 10 more minutes. The dough should still be pale and slightly raw in the center.
9. Melt the butter over a pot over a low heat. Stir in the sugar and combine. Stir in the cream cheese a bit at a time and cook stirring constantly until well incorporated.
10. Add the beaten eggs into the mixture and mix well. Remove from the heat.
11. Spoon the filling in the molds and grill in oven at 220°C (428 °F) for 5-10 minutes until golden brown on top.
12. Take out of the oven and allow to cool.
13. Sprinkle icing sugar on top.

MALLORCAN SNAIL PASTRY Ensaimada

It is the most famous pastry from Mallorca whose origins are debated but are most probably in the Middle East. They are usually enjoyed for breakfast or as an afternoon snack dunked in hot chocolate or coffee when they're not filled, or on their own when they are filled. The most popular filling is pumpkin strands jam (recipe on page 73) but others include whipped cream or almond nougat.

MAKES ABOUT 18 LITTLE ENSAIMADAS
750 gr. (25 oz.) bread flour
15 gr. (3 ¼ tsp.) dry active yeast
4 room temperature eggs
300 ml. (1 ¼ cup) lukewarm milk
180 gr. (3/4 cup) granulated sugar
pinch of salt
200 gr. (7 oz.) vegetable shortening or pork fat to brush
powdered sugar to dust

1. Dissolve the yeast in a bowl with the lukewarm milk.
2. In a large bowl, mix half the flour with the milk/yeast mixture a bit at a time until they form a dough. Cover the bowl with cling film and leave to rise in a warm place until it almost doubles in size, about 1h.
3. Once the dough has risen, add the eggs one at a time using a large wooden spoon or your hands to mix until well incorporated. Mix in the sugar until absorbed. Mix in the remaining flour and salt with your hands until you can form a dough ball. Place on a floured surface and knead for about 4 minutes.
4. Cut it into 18 little dough balls. Knead each one of them and flatten with a dusted rolling pin until 2.5 mm. (0.1 inch) thick.
5. Brush each one of them with a generous amount of vegetable shortening or pork fat and then shape each one of them into a sausage. Allow to rest for 1 hour.
6. Line 2 baking trays with baking paper.
7. Roll each of the dough sausages to make them thinner and longer like a coil or a rope. Place on the baking tray and roll up each coil like a snail leaving 1 cm. (1/3 inch) distance between each bend of the coils and a lot of space between each of the "ensaimadas". You have to take into account the dough will rise and double or triple in size.
8. Place the 2 baking trays in the oven with a cup of water and leave overnight or for at least 10 hours.
9. Pre-heat oven at 180°C (350°F) and cook in middle rack for 10-12 minutes until brown on top. Allow to cool and sprinkle powdered sugar all over the "ensaimadas". They can also be cut lengthwise and filled with Spanish pumpkin strands jam (see recipe on page 73).

CATALAN CRÈME BRÛLÉE

Crema Catalana

This dessert is very similar to the French Crème Brûlée but this one is infused with citrus flavor. It appears regularly on every Spanish restaurant menu and originates from the 18th century when nuns in a convent in Catalonia prepared a flan for a bishop that was too runny. They tried to fix it by adding a layer of burnt sugar and when the Bishop tried it he yelled: "Crema!" meaning in Catalan: "It burns!".

SERVES 4-6
1 liter (4 cups) whole milk
6 large egg yolks
45 gr. (3 Tbsp.) corn flour
half an orange peel
half a lemon peel
1 cinnamon stick
100 gr. (1 cup) granulated sugar +sugar to caramelize

1. Heat the milk with the cinnamon stick, the orange and lemon peel in a saucepan until scalding hot and about to boil. Remove from the heat, cover with a lid and let it set for at least 30 minutes.
2. Separate the eggs, placing the yolks in a large bowl and the whites in a small bowl. You can keep the whites to make other recipes like meringues or omelettes.
3. Whisk the yolks with the sugar until incorporated. Whisk in the corn flour.
4. Pour the milk infusion slowly into the egg mixture in the large bowl, while passing through a sieve. Whisk until well combined. Cook until it thickens.
5. Pour the contents of the bowl into a saucepan and set over a low heat. Stir constantly and scrape the bottom of the pan at the same time with a wooden spatula. Don't let the creme boil because that would ruin it.
6. If you see the creme has curdled or you find bits in it, take the bits out with a sieve spoon or pass the creme through a sieve.
7. Pour into individual containers using a ladle. Refrigerate for at least 4 hours (preferably overnight). The typical containers used in Catalonia are made of clay.
8. Sprinkle a layer of granulated sugar and caramelize with a kitchen torch just before serving.

EGG FLAN Flan de huevo

There's nothing better than finishing a great Spanish meal with this fantastic dessert. It is originally from Spain but has influenced many Latin-American gastronomies. It's a classic and one of the most popular desserts served everywhere in Spain. Beware that the traditional authentic Spanish recipe has no vanilla extract.

SERVES 6-8
4 eggs
4 Tbsp. granulated sugar
500 ml. (2 cups milk)
whipped cream (optional)
6 Tbsp. water
200 gr. (1 cup) granulated sugar for the caramel

1. Pre-heat oven to 190°C (374°F).
2. To make the caramel, bring to a boil 200 gr. (1 cup) of sugar and 3 Tbsp. of water in a saucepan over high heat, without stirring until liquefied and amber in color. While the sugar boils, occasionally brush the inner sides of the pot with water, to keep the sugar from crystallizing.
3. You have 2 options:
   A) Prepare individual flans for each person. You should use ramekins.
   B) Prepare the Flan in one large flan dish.
4. Quickly pour the caramel into the ramekins or flan dish before the caramel gets hard.
5. Break 4 eggs in a large bowl. Beat the eggs with 4 Tbsp. of sugar.
6. Pour in the milk and whisk until smooth with a hand whisk. Pour bowl mixture into the ramekins.
7. Pour water into a large deep baking tray to prepare a "bain mare" boiling water bath. Cover the ramekins with foil and place in the water. The water must cover the bottom half of the ramekins. Bake in pre-heated oven 45-60 min. or until a needle comes out clean when inserted. Be sure to carefully keep the water level topped up while they are in the oven.
8. Let cool at room temperature for 20 minutes. Then chill thoroughly in refrigerator for at least 2 hours. When ready to serve, un-mold by running a knife around the inside edge of each ramekin.
9. Place a plate on top of the ramekin.
10. With one hand under the ramekin and the other on top of the plate, turn over. Tap the ramekin and the flan should drop onto the plate. If it doesn't, carefully "prod" the flan out of the ramekin with a small paring knife. It should slide out.
11. In Spain, it is usually served with whipped cream.

SPANISH CUSTARD Natillas

Homemade Spanish custard is quite different from English custard. The Spanish one is thinner and has a rich tea biscuit on top. Cinnamon is also frequently used which adds a typical Spanish twist. It can keep in the fridge for up to 3 days.

MAKES 4-5
4 egg yolks
2 Tbsp. granulated sugar
1 Tbsp. vanilla sugar
1 Tbsp. corn flour
600 ml. (1 pint) whole milk
ground cinnamon
4 rich tea biscuits or similar

1. Separate the eggs, placing the yolks in a large basin and the whites in a small bowl. You can keep the white to make other recipes like meringues or omelettes.
2. Whisk the yolks. Add the sugar, vanilla sugar and corn flour to the beaten yolks and stir well.
3. Add 2 Tbsp. of milk and whisk into a smooth paste.
4. In a saucepan, heat the remaining milk until scalding hot and about to boil. Pour slowly into the egg mixture in the basin, whisking vigorously as you go.
5. Return it to the saucepan and set over a low heat until it thickens. Stir constantly and scrape the bottom of the pan at the same time with a wooden spatula. Don't let the custard boil because that will ruin it. It'll be ready when the foam around the borders disappears. This can take up to 10 minutes.
6. Pour it into a bowl and let it cool for 10 minutes.
7. If you see the custard has curdled or you find bits in it, take them out with a sieve spoon or pass through a sieve.
8. Pour into individual containers using a ladle. Refrigerate for at least 2 hours.
9. Place the biscuits on top after the custard has refrigerated for 30 minutes. Just before serving, sprinkle ground cinnamon on top.

REFERENCE RECIPES

FISH STOCK Caldo de Pescado

1 liter (4 cups) of water
500 gr. (1 lb.) head, bones and skin of fish
1 leek
1 carrot
1 small onion
½ green bell pepper
2 sprigs of parsley
1 bay leaf
3 Tbsp. Spanish extra virgin olive oil
2 tsp. of sea salt

1. Finely mince the leek, carrot, pepper and onion.
2. Wash the heads, bones and skin of the fish.
3. In a large tall pot with the olive oil, fry the minced vegetables and bay leaf over a medium- low heat. When tender, add in the fish head, bones and skin. Fry for 5 minutes. Stir frequently.
4. Pour in the water. Add the parsley and salt.
5. Simmer uncovered for 20 minutes, skimming off any foam that may form on top.
6. Remove from heat and pass through a sieve.

SEAFOOD STOCK Caldo de Marisco

1 liter (4 cups) of water
1 leek
1 carrot
1 small onion
12 raw unpeeled large shrimps
125 ml (½ cup) of brandy (optional)
3 Tbsp. Spanish extra virgin olive oil
1 tsp. of sea salt

1. Finely mince the leek, onion and carrot.
2. Wash and peel the shrimps with your hands and set aside the heads and shells.
3. Cut the wide part of the shrimps lengthwise to remove the intestines (a black vein). Set aside to use in another shrimp recipe.
4. In large tall pot with olive oil, fry the heads and shells of the shrimps, stirring constantly and pressing the heads down with a wooden spoon so the insides come out. Fry until they have all changed color.
5. Pour in the brandy and cook until alcohol evaporates completely (about 5 minutes or when it stops smelling like alcohol).
6. Pour in the water and season with salt. Add in the minced vegetables.
7. Simmer for 30 minutes,.
8. Remove from heat and pass through a sieve, pressing down the heads so you get out all the liquid inside.

CHICKEN BROTH Caldo de Pollo

2 liters (8 cups) of water
½ medium chicken in pieces
1 leek
2 carrot
1 small onion
2 sprigs of parsley
1 bay leaf
3 Tbsp. Spanish extra virgin olive oil
2 tsp. of sea salt

1. Finely mince the leek, carrots and onion.
2. Wash the chicken pieces making sure there are no guts left. Try to use meat pieces with bones. The more bones, the more taste they will add to the broth. You could even just use one chicken's carcass.
3. In a large tall pot with the olive oil, fry the minced vegetables and bay leaf over a medium- low heat. When tender, add in the chicken pieces. Fry for 10 minutes, stirring frequently.
4. Pour in the water and parsley. Season with salt. Simmer for 1h 30 minutes to 2 hours, skimming off any foam that may form on top.
5. Remove from heat and pass through a sieve.
6. Let it cool in a bowl. After a while, you'll see a layer forming on the surface of the broth. Skim it off as this layer is the chicken's fat.

MAYONNAISE Mayonesa

METHOD 1. BY HAND (SERVES 6-8)
2 egg yolks
½ liter (2 cups) olive oil
½ tsp. vinegar or lemon juice
a pinch of salt

1. Place the egg yolks and salt in a ceramic bowl or mortar. Stir with a whisk, pestle or fork.
2. Then, slowly drizzle a drop of oil while whisking vigorously until you see the oil has been absorbed. Slowly, pour more oil (a small amount) little by little while whisking. Continue drizzling oil and whisking until you've used up all the oil. You'll see how an emulsion starts to form that will turn into mayonnaise at the end.
3. Once it's ready, stir in 1/2 tsp. of vinegar or lemon juice and adjust salt if needed.

METHOD 2. WITH IMMERSION (STICK) BLENDER (SERVES 4)
1 egg at room temperature
1/4 tsp. vinegar or lemon juice
250 ml. (1 cup) olive oil
a pinch of salt

1. Place the egg, olive oil, vinegar and salt in a tall container. Insert the immersion blender switched off in the container. Push the head of the blender onto the bottom and then switch it on, on slow speed. Don't move it for about 5-10 seconds (depending on the blender power).
2. When you see the ingredients turn into a sort of thick mayonnaise (with the immersion blender still on) move the blender slowly up and down until you get a mayonnaise mixture.

EGG AIOLI Allioli con huevo

You can follow any of the 2 Mayonnaise Methods on this page. You just have to add one peeled crushed garlic clove at the beginning of either of the recipes. You can crush it with either a garlic crusher or a mortar and pestle. Do not add any vinegar or lemon juice at the end.

One important tip, if you don't digest raw garlic very well: remove the core by doing the following: Peel the garlic and cut it lengthwise. Insert the knife and remove the small long core that is in the middle. Yes. It´s that simple!

GENUINE AIOLI Allioli

Genuine aioli is made only with garlic, salt and olive oil. It can only be made using a mortar and pestle.

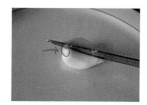

MAKES ABOUT 1 1/2 CUP
10 garlic cloves
a pinch of salt
Spanish extra virgin olive oil

1. Peel the garlic cloves and crush in a mortar with salt. Crush with the pestle until you get a smooth paste.
2. Pour a drop of olive oil slowly into the mortar while you turn the pestle in slow circular motions. When the paste soaks up the oil, pour a very short drizzle of oil while turning the pestle until the paste soaks up the oil again.
3. Pour a longer thin drizzle of oil and repeat turning the pestle. Repeat this process making the drizzle longer each time.
4. It is important that you turn the pestle in wide circular motions while pouring the oil. You will be able to turn the pestle a bit faster everytime you pour olive oil. Keep adding the oil until you have the consistency of a thick mayonnaise. This will take about 20 minutes.

CLASSIC BECHAMEL

This recipe is used for lasagnas, manicotti, cannelloni and other pasta.

1 liter (4 cups) of cold milk
80 gr. (1/2 cup) all purpose flour
80 gr. (5 ½ Tbsp.) olive oil or melted margarine/butter
1 tsp. salt

1. Heat the oil, margarine or butter in a medium size pan or sauce pan over a medium-high heat.
2. Add flour and fry, stirring until mixture is fried (golden), about 1 minute.
3. Add the milk in one go and whisk until smooth. The colder the milk, the less chance of having lumps in the bechamel. Cook over a high heat, whisking until the sauce comes to a boil. Then, reduce to a medium-low heat. Keep on stirring and cook until it thickens (about 6 minutes). Season with salt almost at the end. You want the bechamel to be creamy but not runny. If the bechamel doesn't thicken enough, you can try adding a crushed boiled egg yolk but I recommend frying flour in olive oil in another small pan and adding it into the bechamel. Don't add flour without frying it as the bechamel will taste of uncooked flour.

THICK BECHAMEL

This recipe is used for croquettes and stuffed boiled eggs.

1 liter (4 cups) of cold milk
110 gr. (4 oz.) wheat flour
110 gr. (4 oz.) olive oil or melted margarine/butter
1 tsp. salt

1. Heat the oil, margarine or butter in a medium size pan or sauce pan over a medium-high heat.
2. Add flour and fry, stirring until mixture is fried (golden), for about 1 minute.
3. Add the milk in one go and whisk until smooth. The colder the milk, the less chance of having lumps in the bechamel. Cook over a high heat, whisking until the sauce comes to a boil. Then, reduce to a medium-low heat. Season with salt. Keep on stirring and cook until it thickens enough for a wooden spoon to stand up on its own in the middle of the bechamel sauce. If the bechamel doesn't thicken enough, you can try adding a crushed boiled egg yolk but I recommend frying flour in olive oil in another small pan and adding it into the bechamel. Don't add flour without frying it as the bechamel will taste of uncooked flour.

HARDBOILED EGGS

1. Heat up in a pot or saucepan enough salted water to cover the eggs. Bring to a boil over a high heat and using a spoon, place the eggs one by one into the boiling water. Then, reduce to a medium heat and cook for 10 minutes.
2. Remove the hardboiled eggs with a slotted spoon and place them into a strainer. Chill the eggs by placing them under cold running water for a few seconds.
3. Peel the eggs when they are cool enough to handle and place them on a plate. Take into account that fresher eggs are harder to peel.

MICROWAVE POTATOES

1. Peel and wash 2 large potatoes. Cut them into cubes.
2. Place in a microwave safe casserole dish. Cover the bottom half of the potatoes with tap water. Season with salt and a generous splash of olive oil all over the potatoes.
3. Cover and microwave for 11 minutes or until tender.

Printed by Amazon Italia Logistica S.r.l.
Torrazza Piemonte (TO), Italy

36654566R00047